A CORNISH CHRISTMAS

Christmas at Penelewey.

A CORNISH CHRISTMAS

TONY DEANE & TONY SHAW

The History Press

For (in chronological order)
Kate, Ben, Adam, Hannah, George,
Megan, Poppy, Isobel and Rosie

First published 2025

The History Press
97 St George's Place, Cheltenham,
Gloucestershire, GL50 3QB
www.thehistorypress.co.uk

British Library Cataloguing in Publication Data.
A catalogue record for this book is available from the British Library.

ISBN 978 1 83705 013 0

Typesetting and origination by The History Press.
Printed and bound in Great Britain by TJ Books, Padstow, Cornwall.

MIX
Paper | Supporting responsible forestry
FSC www.fsc.org FSC® C013056

The History Press proudly supports
Trees for Life
www.treesforlife.org.uk

EU Authorised Representative: Easy Access System Europe
Mustamäe tee 50, 10621 Tallinn, Estonia
gpst.request@easproject.com

CONTENTS

THE AUTHORS

Tony Deane and Tony Shaw have both been involved in British traditional culture for well over forty-five years. They wrote *Folklore of Cornwall* in 2003 and have written individually on different aspects of folklore and country life. They were fellow members of the folksong group Legacy in the 1960s and 1970s and, despite their advanced years, continue to sing in folk clubs and at festivals.

ACKNOWLEDGEMENTS

We wish to thank all the writers who have contributed to this collection. While acknowledgements are made in the text, special mention must be given to the following: The extract from *I Would Not Be Forgotten* is reprinted by permission of Tabb House of Padstow © Patrick Hutton, 2004. Virginia Spiers, for actually thanking us for including *In the Brief Midwinter*, a rarity indeed. The extract from *Schoolhouse in the Wind* by Anne Treneer is reprinted by permission of University of Exeter Press, with special thanks to Victoria Owen. The extract from *The Main Cages* is reprinted by permission of Harper Collins Publishers Limited © Philip Marsden, 2002.

We received no other replies to our requests for permission to include extracts but will obviously include full details in any future editions of this book. All unattributed items are by ourselves.

The staff of the Cornish Studies Library at Redruth proved, as ever, to be consistently helpful, while many friends offered useful information and advice: among them were John Buckingham, Jane Coley, Geoff and Fran Doel, Tony Foxworthy, Robert and Ros Husband, Graham O'Callaghan, Doc Rowe, Sally Shaw, Stephanie Smart, Rex Trenouth, David Watts and James Whetter.

We should thank those who provided pictures, particularly Audrey Deane for her photographs. Especial thanks must go to Iris Bishop for transcribing the music and to our families for withstanding the book's gestation period.

To anyone who, in our dotage, we have inadvertently overlooked: our apologies.

Tony Deane, Reigate
Tony Shaw, Penelewey
November 2007

INTRODUCTION

With its unique position on the British mainland it is hardly surprising that many of Cornwall's celebrations are rooted in those local twins: the land and the sea. Some festivals – like Tom Bawcock's Eve in Mousehole – possibly pre-date today's widely accepted meaning of Christmas, while others are firmly of the Christian faith. There is a bleak quality to much of Cornwall's landscape that is, perhaps, at its best in winter and thus overlooked by summer tourists. Padstow's Mummers' Day celebrations, which have attracted such controversy in recent years, are enhanced by the cold: the players seem to spring from the grey streets and bring light to the most grim Boxing and New Year's Days.

In the following collection, we have plundered the works of Hunt, Bottrell and Courtney, nineteenth-century folklorists whose researches form the basis of all who have followed them. We look at far more than folklore, though: here is a cross-section of Christmases old and not so old, from the experiences of both indigenous writers and incomers to Cornwall. Gorran's finest chronicler Anne Treneer rubs shoulders with Robert Stephen Hawker, the eccentric vicar of Morwenstow. That patrician historian Dr A.L. Rowse began life as the son of a china-clay worker and recalls Christmas in Tregonissey in *A Cornish Childhood*, while his near-contemporary and neighbour, the blind and deaf poet

Jack Clemo, describes rare snowfall nearby. There is an extract from Sir Arthur Quiller Couch, better known as 'Q', a writer now sadly neglected, and a poem from the late Charles Causley. Lady Clara Vyvyan and the virtually unknown Mrs John Bonham are among many other visitors to these pages. Ex-patriot Cornishmen are not forgotten, as Oswald Pryor vividly describes Christmas in South Australia.

Perhaps the most vibrant recollections of past Christmases are to be found in contemporary newspaper reports; we have included several here, mostly from the prestigious *West Briton*. Some reveal dark aspects of the past, proving that the 'good old days' were not always so good: the shadow of the workhouse was never far away. Practical joking, too, was prevalent, displaying random cruelty that would not find favour today. There are several nods to the bibulous nature of Yuletide excess, including some previously unpublished reminiscences. Christmas would not be complete without traditional food: there are recipes here, for starrygazy pie and eggy hot, amongst others. To punctuate the text, we have included a selection of carols and secular songs, some familiar, others virtually unknown, but all either unique to or widely sung in Cornwall.

Obviously, this anthology is not comprehensive but we hope that our choices will take you back to the original sources, will whet your appetites for more tastes of Cornish Christmases. Life in Cornwall is becoming more cosmopolitan as, with rising property prices and shortage of employment, many 'locals' move out to be replaced by retired businessmen and second-home owners. So, perhaps, these flashes of what Christmas in Cornwall was and, in some cases, still is like, will encourage a deceleration in the rat race. You could start by visiting Padstow to hear the town's ancient carols during the pre-Christmas week: a haunting sound from a different century.

In general, we have retained punctuation and syntax from the original documents, often eccentric by today's standards, with the Oxford comma flagrant. Setting dialect down on paper is fraught with difficulty and there are inconsistencies here: Q and Rowse were good at it; others less so. We believe that, if not all of these pieces display the highest literary quality, each one contains the spirit of Cornwall and Christmas. They should both be relished.

AUNT MARY

By Robert Stephen Hawker

Robert Stephen Hawker, vicar of Morwenstow from 1835 to 1875, was, perhaps, better known as an eccentric than as a reverend gentleman. He was actually a Devonian, born in Plymouth in 1803 to a clerical family: his father was a doctor who later took holy orders to become vicar of Stratton. Hawker himself was of the high-Anglican persuasion and professed to hate all dissenters but, in fact, his prejudices bowed before his natural generosity of spirit and he gave freely to the poor and sick; he was especially considerate towards those shipwrecked mariners who were frequent, if unwilling, visitors to Morwenstow's treacherous coastline. He died in his home city of Plymouth in 1875, after a deathbed conversion to Roman Catholicism.

As a poet, Hawker was talented but didactic. Yet, through the miasma of religious pedantry, shone several gems: the unfinished Arthurian epic *Quest of the Sangraal*, which Tennyson considered a serious rival to his *Idylls of the King; Song of the Western Men*, better known as *Trelawney* and now regarded as the traditional Cornish national anthem; and the piece featured below. This is headed by an extract from *I Would Not Be Forgotten* (2004), Patrick Hutton's excellent critical study of Hawker's life and work; the poem is a

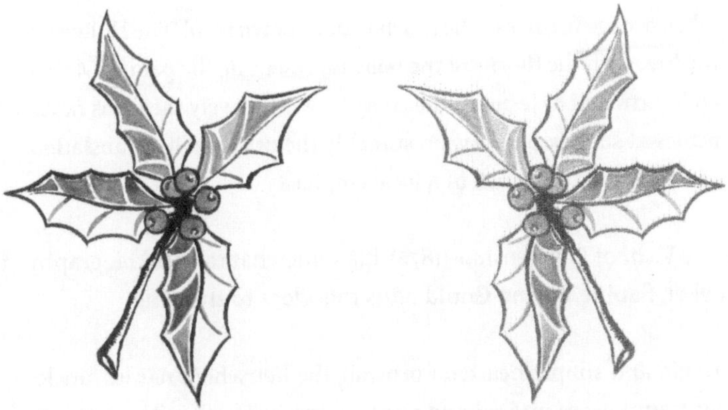

reworking of *The Holly and the Ivy* theme, which Hawker subtitled *A Christmas Chant*. Tony Deane wrote the tune.

'Modryb Marya – Aunt Mary' (1838) provides a welcome antidote to all that carping about Dissenters, offering as it does a warmth and simplicity to match the relationship that Hawker hoped to establish with his new parishioners. With its cheerful rhythm, and slightly varied refrain that so well suits a carol, it takes as its theme the symbolism of the holly tree in Christian folklore, embracing the hedgerow's uniquely bright bounty at Christmas, there for everyone including the poor. It is also evergreen, emblematic of eternal life, and spattered with berries, like blood falling from the crucified body of Christ onto his mother standing below. Meanwhile the robin, his breast reddened by the same source, sings on Christmas Eve, and shelter is given to all the birds especially on Christmas Day. There is a hint of the poet's favourite habit of equating birds with angels, '*Ubi aves ibi angeli*', where birds are, there are angels. The name 'Aunt Mary's Tree' becomes entirely appropriate. The same symbolism is taken a stage further in the much better known carol 'The Holly and the Ivy', with the thorns of the holly representing the pain of Mary's childbirth and of Jesus on the cross. Hawker's lovely carol has never achieved such popularity. Presumably the title, and his translation of it, provides too much of a local emphasis.

In *The Vicar of Morwenstow* (1876), his somewhat fanciful biography of Hawker, Sabine Baring-Gould adds this gloss to the song:

> In old and simple-hearted Cornwall, the household names 'uncle' and 'aunt' were uttered and used as they are to this day in many countries of the East, not only as phrases of kindred, but as words of kindly greeting and tender respect. It was in the spirit, therefore, of this touching and graphic usage, that they were wont, on the Tamar side, to call the Mother of God, in their loyal language, *Modryb Marya*, or Aunt Mary.

Now of all the trees by the king's highway,
Which do you love the best?
O! the one that is green upon Christmas Day,
The bush with the bleeding breast.
Now the holly with her drops of blood for me:
For that is our dear Aunt Mary's tree.

Its leaves are sweet with our Saviour's Name,
'Tis a plant that loves the poor:
Summer and winter it shines the same,
Beside the cottage door.
O! the holly with her drops of blood for me:
For that is our kind Aunt Mary's tree.

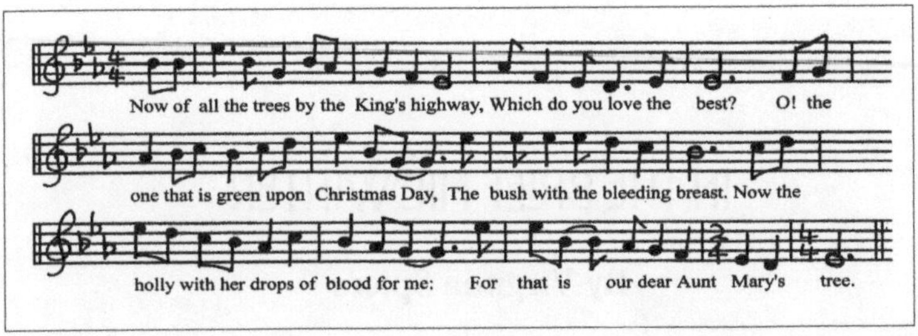

'Tis a bush that the birds will never leave:
They sing in it all day long;
But sweetest of all upon Christmas Eve,
Is to hear the robin's song.
'Tis the merriest sound upon earth and sea:
For it comes from our own Aunt Mary's tree.

So, of all that grow by the king's highway,
I love that tree the best;
'Tis a bower for the birds upon Christmas Day,
The bush of the bleeding breast.
O! the holly with her drops of blood for me:
For that is our sweet Aunt Mary's tree.

IN THE BRIEF MIDWINTER

By Virginia Spiers

The Guardian newspaper includes a Country Diary in each edition. Here is the entry for 29 December 2004, written by Virginia Spiers, from the Tamar Valley:

> In the gloomy, short days of midwinter, brief spells of sun are at a premium, gilding the tops of bare trees and emerald fields in the Tamar's steep tributaries. Sunbeams glint off ivy, holly and harts tongue; haloes shine around mossy branches and, in sunken lanes, midday shadows reach towards the tops of banks thick with pennyworts. On clear nights, stars compete with urban glow and rural house lights, supplemented now with flashing garlands, luminous snowmen, electric icicles and reindeer with Father Christmas.
>
> Towards a more sparsely populated part of the south coast, dampness enhances the marzipan smell of winter heliotrope beside Lansallos churchyard and the slippery path towards the grey sea and elusive horizon. Jackdaws flock across the stepped and buttressed cliffs clad in ivy and bracken almost to sea level. Tufted lichens on Pencarrow Head, yellow-lichened elder and brilliant gorse flowers contrast with blackthorn scrub. Grazing sheep and ponies trample and help control rank vegetation above Lantic Bay.

Midwinter.

A couple of violets beside the muddy path hint at next year's spring, and orange-berried stinking-iris thrive with stunted sycamores by Blackbottle headland. The Gribbin is blurry and closer, just across the Fowey Estuary, Readymoney Cove is shrouded in drizzle.

Before Christmas, Polruan seemed almost deserted, holiday cottages in its narrow streets shut up and dark. Upstream, by Pont Pill's vacant moorings, rain drips through old oaks on to holly berries and hazel catkins. Uphill, the tower of Lanteglos church is a pale grey silhouette and the narrow roads are awash.

MOUSEHOLE ON TOM BAWCOCK'S EVE

We were commissioned to write the original edition of *Folklore of Cornwall* in 1974. Twenty-nine years passed before the work was updated and this extract comes from the new version, amended to include the full text and tune of *Tom Bawcock's Eve*. The song was created from surviving fragments by Robert Morton Nance, once Grand Bard of the Cornish Gorsedd, early in the last century and set to a Cornish dance-tune called *The Wedding March*. It was printed in Ralph Dunstan's *Cornish Dialect and Folk Songs* in 1932. The dialect words translate as follows: *morgy* - dog-fish; *lances* – sand-eels; *scad* – horse-mackerel; *fairmaids* – pilchards; *oozles* – throats; *clunk* – swallow.

In Mousehole, on 23 December, the fisherfolk celebrate Tom Bawcock's Eve. The day is said to commemorate a period of local famine eased by the brave efforts of one fisherman, Tom Bawcock (or Bowcock), who put to sea in a dreadful storm and returned with seven different varieties of fish to feed the starving villagers. The little port is bathed in colour for Tom Bawcock's Eve, as both the buildings around the harbour and the boats in it are hung with Christmas lights. After a character dressed as Tom, with a mock

boat attached to his waist, processes with musicians to the Ship Inn, portions of starrygazy pie, with fish-heads poking through the crust, are handed out to customers. A song, restored in the 1920s by Robert Morton Nance, accompanies the proceedings:

A merry place, you may believe,
was Mousehole 'pon Tom Bawcock's Eve:
To be there then who wouldn't wish to sup on seven sorts of fish?

When morgy brath had cleared the path comed lances for a fry
And then us had a dish o' scad and starrygazy pie.

Chorus.

Next comed fairmaids, braw thusty jades, as made our oozles dry,
And ling and hake, enough to make a running shark to sigh.

Chorus.

As each were clunk his health was drunk in bumpers brimming high
And when up came Tom Bawcock's name we praised un to the sky.

Chorus.

The festival's origins perhaps had deeper significance than the quelling of hunger: Bawcock could be derived from the Cornish mow-cock, '*cock fair*', or the French *beau coq*, 'the cock of St Peter'. A village dance in nearby St Just-in-Penwith was called *The Cock Dance* and, in antiquity, the cock was regarded as the sun's sacred herald, while the fish was a fertility symbol.

The Mousehole Cat, a book for children written by Antonia Barber in 1990, illustrated by Nicola Bayley and later produced as an animated film, tells Tom Bawcock's story and the memory of his heroic voyage lives on in his home village. Only once in recent years was he forgotten. In the terrible aftermath of the Penlee Lifeboat disaster of 1981, when eight men of Mousehole – among them Charlie Greenhaugh, then landlord of the Ship Inn – perished, a greater courage than Tom's took precedence and the lights in Mousehole harbour were dimmed.

There are various versions of starrygazy (or stargazy) pie, a dish on the permanent menu at the Ship Inn in Mousehole. Here is one from Sally Shaw's collection:

To serve 6.
shortcrust pastry, made with 285g plain flour;
8 pilchards, sardines or small herrings;
salt, pepper;
1 large chopped onion;
approx 3 tbsps chopped parsley;
3 hard-boiled eggs;
3 rashers streaky bacon;
beaten eggs to glaze.

Roll out the pastry for double-crust plate pie.
Cover the plate, brush the rim with water and roll out another piece for the lid. Keep it aside.

Preheat the oven to Gas Mark 6 (200°c, 400°f).

Clean and bone the fish, leaving their heads in place.

Season inside and stuff with finely-chopped onion and parsley. Fold back into shape.

Lay the fish on the pastry like the spokes of a wheel with their heads on the rim so that they can gaze upwards. Fill the gaps in between with chopped bacon and hard-boiled eggs.

Put the pastry lid in place, pressing down between the fish heads so that it meets the pastry of the lower rim, making a wavy effect. Brush with beaten egg.

Bake for 30 minutes, though if the fish are large allow 15 minutes more at the reduced heat of Gas Mark 4 (180°c, 350°f).

Serve hot.

Although Mousehole exemplifies the custom of decorating Cornwall's harbours with Christmas lights, it is not unique: the lights at Padstow, Mevagissey, Coverack, Newlyn, Cadgwith, Penzance and Porthleven are among the similarly impressive. Denis Atherton wrote in *The Guardian* for 23 December 1995, that:

> Summer visitors to picturesque Cornish fishing harbours would not give a passing thought to Christmas light displays. But hardly has the last caravan disappeared over the Tamar Bridge than the fishing communities set about the task of flooding their villages with a rainbow of seasonal colour.

He described the favourite displays of sea-serpents and spouting whales, then continued:

> Ashore, house windows and shop fronts are lit up. And the light and the colour rises up the steep backdrop of the fishing villages in a kaleidoscope that would astonish the summer visitor more used to thinking of Cornwall's pretty harbours in terms of sand, rocks and sunshine.
>
> The custom of Christmas lights has its roots in the misty Cornish tradition of a candle in the window to guide the seamen safely home. In Victorian times, most fishermen's cottages sported a Christmas candle throughout the festive season, though the vogue for the modern, extravagant displays dates mostly from the 1960s.

In the few years since these words were written, Cornwall's holiday season has extended to be more or less the year round. The Christmas lights are now a must for many visitors.

OUR CORNWALL

By C.C. Vyvyan

Clara Coltman Vyvyan was born in Australia but moved to her ancestral home of Cornwall when she was two years old. She wrote several topographical books under her maiden name of C.C. Rogers, before, in 1929, marrying Colonel Sir Courtney Vyvyan, the tenth baronet of Trelowarren. She continued her literary career with works such as *Gwendra Cove, From a Cornish Window* and, in 1948, *Our Cornwall*, from which the following charming extract is taken:

> Christmas Day was usually rather quiet and even on Christmas Eve there was little extra movement in the village save for the bringing in to Churchtown of evergreens and holly for the Christmas decorations. Mr Baragwanath from a time unreckoned had always done the pulpit, but every year he would gain fresh glory by balancing a lamb of cotton-wool upon the summit and placing in that uncouth but symbolic figure a holly-berry for each eye. That same lamb would serve at Easter with two buttons from a lady's boot. Mrs Dave Chynoweth 'belonged to' do the font, but she was too artistic to repeat a design and every year she rang the changes in arrangement of her evergreens; but one year she surpassed herself in ingenuity

and patience, and that was the year when she crowned the font with a bush of furze, whitewashed all over, and as substitute for the golden blooms there was a holly berry stuck upon each thorn. There were eleven little Chynoweths, each one of an age to prick its finger.

SNOWFALL AT KERNICK

By Jack Clemo

Goonamarris Slip lies in the centre of the china-clay country, north of St Austell: a stark uncompromising district meriting the soubriquet 'The Cornish Alps' only from a distance. There, Jack Clemo was born in 1916. He became partially, then profoundly, deaf in his youth and lost his sight in1955. These disabilities perhaps sharpened his writing skills, his intense personal reflections. His early novels, notably *Wilding Graft* (1948), were heavily influenced by Thomas Hardy and the Powys brothers but his poetry was uniquely individual, a product of his environment. He married late in life and moved to Dorset but his poems, although softer, remained rooted in Cornish clay. He died in 1994.

This graphic work first appeared in *The Clay Verge* (1951):

Here with a burly flutter and sting
The snow-blast scampers winnowing,
And dribble of foam-flakes seeps and bores
Through clay-clump thickets, under doors;
While flurry of snow-mist rises where
The waggons tug till rails are bare.

Snowfall at Kernick.

The smoke is battered round the stacks;
Soot falls with snow on trolley-tracks.
Even the mica-channel planks
And narrow walls of settling-tanks
Are frilled and ice-splashed there between
The frozen pools now sickly green.
The pit-edge merges with the fields,
A softened gash the clay-bone shields;
Beyond it in the valley's fold
Virginia woods loom taut and cold.

Snow is rare enough in Cornwall and, especially, the Isles of Scilly to provoke newspaper coverage. The *West Briton* for Christmas Day, 1835, reported:

> Winter seems at length to have decidedly set in amongst these islands (Scilly). On Saturday night there was a heavy fall of snow (an unusual occurrence here) and the weather, since, has been severely cold, with a strong easterly wind, which has already blown in above a hundred vessels to the different anchorages.

CHRISTMAS SHOPPING

Overspending and flamboyance at Christmas are not modern phenomena, as these two extracts from *Old Penzance* (1956) by Edgar A. Rees show:

> Naturally many changes in the observance of Christmas around Penzance have occurred during the last sixty years. Prior to this period as the 25th drew near the shop windows in the town took on quite a 'new look' to their usual routine. The most noticeable feature was the number and character of the novelties exhibited in the windows of the various streets. Foremost among them was to be seen, year after year, in Jimmy Runnals' pork shop on the Terrace, high up in the window – inside and out – pigs' heads with a jet of gas flaming from their mouths; others having an orange or lemon placed in them. Simpson's the Tailors could be relied upon to produce a realistic jungle scene with either a fierce-looking lion or tiger looking out from its lair. On one occasion the Penzance Clothing Company, whose premises at that time were immediately below the present National Provincial Bank, exhibited a wonderful mechanical toy – first of its kind to be shown in the town – showing 'Wrastlers in a bout'. The various hitches displayed by the lively little figures were so very realistic as to draw the crowds of men,

women and children who remained watching the antics of the toy, causing serious obstruction in this narrow street to both wheeled and foot traffic. So much so that, eventually, the novelty had, on police orders, to be removed from the window.

The displays made by the confectioners in their windows were real works of art, especially at Hamlyn's in Chapel Street, where 'raffles' for the large iced cakes were a feature on Christmas Eve. In fact 'raffles' were the order of the day in most of the shops in the town during the festival period.

The paper chains used to decorate the houses were, of course, home-made. Weeks prior to Christmas the young folk could be seen in the evenings busily engaged in cutting out narrow strips of coloured tissue paper with a pair of scissors, whilst others formed them into long chains by the aid of a mixture of flour and water.

For the basis of the Christmas tree large-sized wooden hoops were largely used and from which dangled little pottery figures representing Father Christmas, tubby policemen, etc, that danced at the end of an elastic tag. Small Chinese paper lanterns illuminated the tree after dark.

Children's parties were, of course, looked forward to from Boxing Day to the end of January. The games then in vogue at these parties were first and foremost Postman's Knock, Blindman's Buff, Hunt the Slipper, Musical Chairs, Spin the Platter, Pork and Greens, Treasure Hunt and, the great favourite, Family Coach.

The scene in Penzance on Christmas Eve was indeed an unforgettable one; the streets being crowded to capacity with folks who flocked in to the bright lights of the town from the neighbouring villages, making it difficult to move around with any degree of comfort. The brightly-lit and attractive shops being crammed to the doors with last-minute customers up to 11 o'clock, some of the shops not

> putting up their shutters till midnight. Bands played favourite carol music, and different 'Curl' parties singing in selected pitches. Public houses kept open from 7 am to 10 pm.

We will look at Christmas sports and games later but, for now, back to the shopkeepers of old Penzance:

> It was the practice of the Penzance butchers who had stalls in the old meat market to assemble outside the entrance at the close of day, on Christmas Eve, and render a fine selection of carols. Having regard to the standard of music in those days when there were no male voice choirs as at present, the singing of the Penzance butchers was very good indeed, and large crowds of people gathered around to hear them. Most of the villages in the neighbourhood could boast of excellent 'Curl' parties. About 1860 the men and boys of the Mousehole Wesleyan Chapel choir always formed themselves into a carol party on the approach of Christmas. They were under the leadership of Richard Barnes who led the trebles with a violin. Mr Bond, of Newlyn, led the altos with a flute. James Harvey, the tenors with another violin, and George Barnes (father of the leader) led the basses with a bass viol. This choir left Mousehole at midnight on Christmas Eve and proceeded to Paul. After singing in the church-town they visited Trevithal, Halwyn, and Raginnis in turn. At some of the houses they were invited to sing indoors, being regaled with Christmas cake and coffee; at others they were listened to from open windows.

When, in the early 1970s, we were asked to write *The Folklore of Cornwall* we received many letters written, it was obvious, by purse-lipped correspondents doubting the wisdom of such a venture. There had been far too many such books, they explained, for yet another to have any chance of success. In fact, the most recent substantial book dedicated solely to Cornish folklore was M.A. Courtney's *Cornish Feasts and Folk-Lore*, published in 1890. Margaret Ann Courtney, born in Penzance in 1834, was a poet and antiquarian who gathered her material from the eminent folklorists Robert Hunt and William Bottrell and from the pages of *Notes and Queries*. She died in 1920. The following is the first of many from her work that will appear in this book:

> At Falmouth the lower classes formerly expected from all the shopkeepers, of whom they bought any of their Christmas groceries, a slice of cake and a small glass of gin. Some of the oldest established tradespeople still observe this custom, but it will soon be a thing of the past.

It was already 'a thing of the past' in Launceston if this notice which appeared in the *East Cornwall Times* for Saturday 17 December 1859 is to be believed:

> The inhabitants of Launceston and the public generally are respectfully informed that we the undersigned grocers of Launceston approving of the agreements of the tradesmen of the neighbouring towns do hereby unanimously agree to abolish the practice of giving what is usually called 'Christmasing' the custom being very unsatisfactory.
> Signed: Doidge & Nicholls, Jos Splittigue, J T Planse, J Powell.

A.K. Hamilton Jenkin, of whom more later, described in *Cornish Homes and Customs* (1934) how the country poor bypassed shopkeepers for their Christmas charity:

> In the towns it is customary for old women, commonly known as 'Christmas widows' to visit their well-to-do neighbours at this time to gather money or ingredients for their 'bit of Chrestmus cake'. This is generally known as 'going a-gooding', and is still observed in Redruth, as doubtless in other places.

As social conditions have improved, such a practice would be frowned upon today but, with twenty-four-hour opening becoming more common, the shopworker may look with envy at this report from the *West Briton* for 23 December 1853:

> We stated last week that Mr N Gill, of Truro, draper, had announced his intention of closing his shop on the Monday after Christmas day, and we suggested that the example should be generally followed in Truro and other towns in the county. We are glad that this is about to be carried into effect. The booksellers, druggists, and shoemakers of Truro, have agreed to close their shops on Monday next, and a bill has been issued from the Mayor recommending a general holiday, which will no doubt be attended to. At St Austell the shopkeepers, not wishing to be behind those in other towns, have agreed to close their shops on Monday next. At St Ives the drapers have unanimously agreed to give their assistants a holiday on Monday the 26th instant, and to close their shops at 5 o'clock each evening for the remainder of the week. At Penzance there will be a suspension of business on Monday next, and an early closing of the drapers' shops on Tuesday and Wednesday.

The beneficent Mr Gill opened his drapery business in 1833 and it continued until 1954 when the prominent site in Boscawen Street was taken over by F.W. Woolworth.

Christmas celebrations in Truro.

CHRISTMAS FARE

While food and Christmas remain synonymous, today's standards of hygiene would not respond well to this report of Truro Market from the *West Briton* of 28 December 1837:

> Our meat market on Saturday last did not present so fine an appearance as it is usual on Christmas occasions. The general character of the beef, though good, being far from what is usually dominated prime. The poultry market was, however, well supplied, the geese especially being numerous and fine; but in consequence of the smallness of the room, the heat occasioned by the dense crowd was so great that the fat on some of them was literally melting and the inconvenience to both buyers and sellers was almost insufferable.

The influx of exotic foods is nothing new, as these two notices from the same newspaper reveal:

> FOR SALE: About 900 frails of Figs just landed from Lisbon and are in excellent order. Francis S Symonds (Merchant) Falmouth. (21/12/1810)

> TURKEYS: On Monday about 300 Turkeys were brought to the Redruth Railway Station. Each bird was weighed and ticketed at

> the Market Place which attracted a great crowd. The birds were in fine condition. (24/12/1877)

Margaret Courtney described a favourite Christmas pie in Cornwall, that land of pies:

> A sweet giblet pie was one of the standing dishes at a Christmas dinner – a kind of mince-pie, into which the giblets of a goose, boiled and finely chopped, were put instead of beef.

She also revelled in the importance of cakes, quoting from George C. Boase in *Notes and Queries* for 21 December 1878:

> In some parts of the county it is customary for each household to make a batch of currant cakes on Christmas-eve. These cakes are made in the ordinary manner, coloured with saffron, as is the custom in these parts. On this occasion the peculiarity of the cakes is, that a small portion of the dough in the centre of each top is pulled up and made into a form which resembles a very small cake on the top of a large one, and this centre-piece is usually called 'the Christmas'. Each person in a house has his or her especial cake, and every person ought to taste a small piece of every other person's cake. Similar cakes are also bestowed on the hangers-on of the establishment, such as laundresses, sempstresses, charwomen, &c.; and even some people who are in the receipt of weekly charity call, as a matter of course, for their Christmas cakes. The cakes must not be cut until Christmas-day, it being probably 'unlucky to eat them sooner'.
>
> The material to make these and nearly all the cakes at this season were at one time given by the grocers to their principal customers.

Stirring the Christmas pudding

Perhaps Christmas cakes were so popular because, in Cornwall, they generally contained a fair amount of whisky and orange juice. Christmas puddings, too, were enhanced by alcohol, often port wine. A Cornish superstition states that 'the more you taste of various Christmas puddings, the greater will be the number of happy days during the following year'.

However, the eating of cakes had to come to an end, as Miss Courtney stressed:

> All Christmas-cakes must be eaten by the end of Twelfth-tide, as it is unlucky to have any left, and all decorations must be taken down on the next day, because for every forgotten leaf of evergreen a ghost will be seen in the house in the course of the ensuing year. This latter superstition does not prevail, however, in all parts of Cornwall, as in some districts a small branch is kept to scare away evil spirits.

Of course, not all the people could enjoy fine fare. Miss Courtney, again:

> A very general (meal) for poor people in some parts of the county on Christmas-eve was pilchards and unpeeled potatoes boiled together in one 'crock'.

One can only wonder how appropriate was the word 'abundance' when the West Briton in 1876 reported that the patients of Cornwall Lunatic Asylum in Bodmin were, 'regaled on Christmas Day with an abundance of roast Geese and Pork, Plum Pudding, Etc'. The same paper offered this somewhat patronising portrait of Christmas in Truro Workhouse in its edition for 27 December 1867:

> It is gratifying to know that while every family that could afford it were enjoying the good things with which Christmas is celebrated, the large and unfortunate family, consisting of the aged and infirm,

> the destitute and helpless, now in our workhouse, were not forgotten. On Christmas day, the inmates, to the number of 255, were supplied with a dinner of roast beef and plum pudding, and after they had partaken of these to their full content, the old men were treated to what to many of them was a real luxury, pipes and tobacco, the old women with snuff with which to tickle their olfactory nerves; and the children with oranges and nuts. In the evening they were all provided with a bountiful supply of excellent cake and tea. It is scarcely necessary to say that the whole was greatly enjoyed. The dining hall had been most profusely and tastefully festooned and decorated with evergreens and artificial flowers, interspersed with Chinese variegated lamps, by the superintendent of labour and the porter, and its appearance in the evening when lighted by the coloured lamps, was strikingly brilliant and pleasing.

During the next nine years, temperance seems to have deserted the workhouse: here is another report from the *West Briton*, this time from 28 December 1876:

> The inmates of the workhouse, 192 in number, had their usual treat of roast beef and plum pudding for dinner on Christmas day; also currant cake and sugar and tea for supper. Those inmates who liked had beer with their dinner (children excepted), those who did not care for beer had either tea or cocoa; this is a new feature, henceforth those who did not care for beer had nothing.

Employers and local gentry also offered benevolence to the poor. In 1877, paupers from the parishes adjacent to Menabilly, near Fowey, received, 'on Christmas Eve, the usual supply of beef and bread for their Christmas dinners'; each person was given one shilling. Six years later, the *Cornish Times* reported that:

> On Christmas Eve the mayor of Liskeard (Mr W Polkinghorne) gave a tea in the town hall to 200 poor people in the town. The volunteer band was present and rendered festive music.

Continuing an established practice, Copperhouse Foundry treated its employees to Christmas largesse in 1843, according to the *West Briton* for 29 December that year:

> Messrs Sandys, Carne and Vivian, of Hayle, lately distributed to the workmen in their establishments, according to annual custom, in lieu of what is commonly called a 'way-goose dinner', the following sums: To each man, 4s (20p); to each young man, 3s6d (17½p); to each lad, 3s (15p); to each boy, 2s6d (12½p). This method is highly to be recommended, as it enables the receiver to use the gift in the manner best suited to his wants. A dinner was provided for their agents.

On 2 January 1846, the *West Briton* (again) presented this picture of the charitable gentry:

> Sir Wm Trelawney, Bart, Lord Lieutenant of this county, has rejoiced the hearts of the poor of Calstock, and its neighbourhood, by his liberal and seasonable gifts.
>
> Lady Basset caused two fat bullocks to be slaughtered on Christmas Eve, and distributed, together with several sacks of flour, among the poor of the parish of Illogan.
>
> Philip Vyvyan Robinson, Esq, late of Nansloe, but now of Tehidy, has ordered to be distributed among (as he calls them) his poorer neighbours at the top of Meneage-street, Helston, a large quantity of coals.
>
> W A H Arundell, Esq, of Trebursye House, near Launceston, generously distributed a large quantity of blankets, last week, among the poor of South Petherwin.

George W Webber, Esq, of Hexworthy House, Launceston, last week made his annual presentation of beef, bread and wood, to the poor families of the parish of Lawhitton.

On Christmas Eve, six hundredweights of prime beef and a large quantity of bread, were distributed to the poor of Tywardreath; and one guinea (£1.05) and a quantity of warm clothing to each of twenty deserving widows, being the annual munificent gift of Wm Rashleigh, Esq, of Menabilly.

A.K. Hamilton Jenkin was born in Redruth in 1900 and educated at Sherborne, Clifton and University College, Oxford. At the latter, he became friends with C.S. Lewis and later, in 1927, was a founder Bard of the Cornish Gorsedd. Before his death in 1980, he was recognised as one of Cornwall's foremost social and industrial historians. This extract is taken from *Cornish Homes and Customs*, published in 1934, although he is quoting from the nineteenth-century writer William Bottrell. The importance of hunting would shock our politically correct age, while vegetarians would shrink from most of the food. A 'crowd', incidentally, which Hamilton Jenkins translates as a tambourine, was, we believe, a violin. So now we return to the gentry:

The 'Twelve Days of Christmas' was a phrase which meant much to the Cornish people of old who, were they to come to life again, would find in our modern Christmas but a faint echo of the mirth and joy with which they celebrated this period of the year. Nowhere in the pages of Dickens himself will a more satisfying picture be found of Christmas cheer than that given by Bottrell of the way in which this day was formerly kept by the Lovell family at their old mansion of Trewoofe (Trove), near Penzance.

Long before daylight on the Christmas morning the women of the household were up and busy with the preparation of the pies, meat, game, and poultry, and all the roasting, boiling, and baking which had to be done in readiness for the feast. Before the break of dawn, too, the men themselves had left the hall, and the valleys and hills resounded to the winding of the bugle horn which roused the neighbouring villages to join in the hunting and hare-tracing over the newly-fallen snow. As soon as the men were gone, the great open fireplace in the hall was filled from end to end with logs of oak, ash, and elm, and sweet-smelling bog-turf laid between. Before this great fire were placed the spits on which were roasted the huge joints of meat, whilst woodcock, snipe, plover, teal and other game were cooked in the dripping-pans beneath. Meantime, the kitchen chimney and oven were taken up with pies of every sort, pigeon, poultry, giblet, rabbit, hare, mullet, bass, veal, besides those of parsley and sweet herbs. In addition to all these were puddings, pasties, cakes, and other knick-knacks designed to tempt the more delicate appetites. About midday the squire, with some of the elderly hunters and the ladies who had been up on the hills to see the chase, would return home; the table was then laid, and from that time till long after dark company after company kept coming in laden with the game and 'hungry as hounds'.

Splendid indeed the old house must have looked at such times – with its branches of holly, box, and bay; garlands of ivy on window and wall; and the great burnished candlesticks standing on the table between steaming bowls and tankards, piles of apples roasted and raw, and the heaps of sweet cakes. Long after the weary attendants had retired to bed and the ladies themselves had tucked up their fine dresses and fallen with right good will to the task of serving, the feasting continued. At length the company, weary of 'eating the good things to save them', fell to dancing to tunes beaten out on pewter and brass pans, and the strains of the 'crowd' (tambourine). Daylight had often come before the party at last broke up amidst cheers for the squire, the draining of stirrup cups, and voices bidding a 'Merry Christmas and a Happy New Year to one and all'.

Welcome Christmas which brings us all good cheer,
Pies and puddings, roast pork and strong beer.
Chorus: Come let me taste your Christmas beer
That is so very strong,
And I do wish that Christmas time
With all its mirth and song
Was twenty times so long.

So ran the opening verse of one of those quaint old secular carols for which the county has long been famous, and which so admirably expressed the sentiments of those who formerly sang them.

Long, indeed, before the modern world has even begun to consider the approach of Christmas, the old people would be engaged in deciding upon the all-important question of the 'curl' (carol) singing which formed such a prominent feature of this festive season. Printed copies of these carols being almost unknown, the singers had either to write out their own parts in MS, or where, as was frequently the case, the choirs consisted entirely of persons who were unable to read musical notation, the parts themselves had to be memorized. All this entailed strenuous work, and as the Christmastide approached, longer and longer became the sessions and more and more arduous the practices; for the leader, generally some old man chosen by mutual consent, was hard to please, and would have everything done just 'fitty' or not at all. Eleven o'clock or more had often come before the various bands broke up, and on their way homewards their voices might still be heard raising the fine old melodies with which their forefathers had wakened those selfsame lanes and rugged moorlands for centuries before them.

A week or so before Christmas the arrival of the 'curl' singers was eagerly awaited in the towns and villages, and the surrounding farms. Then, on some dark night, when the family were seated before the fire blazing cheerfully on the open hearth, shuffling footsteps would be heard in the outer kitchen, accompanied by the scraping of throats and a voice giving directions in a stage whisper. A minute afterwards a question from the leader: 'Are 'ee ready, boys?' would be followed by the order: 'Sound for it, then!' and the voices would be raised in a long-drawn-out 'do-o-o', to try the pitch. This preliminary accomplished, the leader would hastily call forth in a sort of chanting tone the first line of the carol:

As I sat on a sunny bank.

At the word 'bank' the whole choir took up their parts and burst forth in full harmony from the beginning.

AS I SAT ON A SUNNY BANK

As a variant of *I Saw Three Ships*, perhaps dating from the fifteenth century, this carol is not unique to Cornwall, although it is especially popular there. Performed as a shanty – with the 'story' lines sung solo and the responses in chorus – this succinct version was collected in St Buryan by Tony Deane in 1965 and has not previously been published.

As I sat on a sunny bank,
On Christmas Day, on Christmas Day,
As I sat on a sunny bank,
On Christmas Day in the morning.
I saw three ships come sailing in,
I saw three ships come sailing in.

And who should be in those ships three,
But Joseph and his fair lady?

And he did whistle and she did sing,
And all the bells on earth did ring.

And all the world cried out for joy,
That they had seen the holy boy.

Then let us all rejoice again,
O let us all rejoice again.

I saw three ships come sailing in,
I saw three ships come sailing in.

AUSTRALIA'S LITTLE CORNWALL

By Oswald Pryor

Hamilton Jenkin remarked that 'the Cornish people not only rejoiced in their carols when at home, but introduced them wherever they were scattered in the New World or the Old'. North of Adelaide, in South Australia, the 'Copper Triangle' includes the towns of Moonta, Woolaroo and Kadina. When copper was discovered there in the 1840s, many Cornish tin-miners emigrated to make their fortunes. A good number succeeded and the families remained in the area after the mines' final closures in the 1920s. Today, Cornish names abound and the terrain closely resembles the Poldice Valley in Cornwall: dead, bleak land broken by crumbling engine houses. Oswald Pryor was born at Moonta Mines to Cornish parents: he became a prominent cartoonist working for Australian newspapers and wrote his definitive account of Australia's Little Cornwall in 1962:

> Carol singing by candlelight is now an Australian institution. Every year, a few days before Christmas, thousands of people gather on park lawns, each carrying a lighted candle, to sing programmes of sacred songs. The custom is supposed to have started in Melbourne

in 1938 and to have spread to other centres of population, but as far back as 1865 the Cornish miners of Moonta were singing carols by the light of 'fatjacks' – tallow candles – stuck on the front of their safety hats with dabs of damp clay.

The Christmas Eve shift was a short one, and during it the men were not inclined to work at the face of the lode. They gathered on the shaft plats, or loading platforms, to 'give un lip', and the captains turned a blind eye – although they couldn't turn a deaf ear – to the fact that the men were singing carols instead of working.

The songs were those which their cockfighting, smuggling ancestors had sung after they had found grace during the great revival brought about by the visits of John Wesley and his followers to Cornwall in the middle of the eighteenth century. The tunes of the Cornish carols are characterized by florid airs, a rolling bass and frequent points of imitation. Words are from the psalters and from nonconformist hymn books, with a few lyrics by local composers. Singing in the chapels was accompanied by instrumentalists who played flutes, ophicleides, serpents, and bassoons. On one occasion seven bassoons played the bass and a local critic declared: 'When they all closed down on low F, 'twas like 'eaven!'

Outside critics of the carols alleged that the tunes ignored all the rules of harmony, that there was a monotonous sameness about them, and that the working miners who composed them merely cribbed from each other. But the Cousin Jacks ignored such comments. Their 'curls' were among their most cherished possessions, and at Christmas they were the basis of a musical festival.

Hundreds walked miles to attend the 6.30 services on Christmas morning. In little chapels decorated with boughs of evergreens, and throughout the rest of the day and the following one itinerant parties moved around to sing carols in the better homes, in hotel bars, and on street corners. The local band played in Captain Hancock's

Mines at St Agnes.

garden before breakfast, and children went from door to door, singing for pennies. Parties of young fellows entered cottages whose doors had been left open, drank 'swanky' home-brew, and kept on singing until after midnight. In intervals between carols they recalled other Christmases, such as the one when a local counterpart of Ebenezer Scrooge had locked his door, and when a party of singers called had refused to open it. 'What say, boys?' the leader of the party asked his mates, 'Shall us give 'un verse of 'Ark, 'Ark (*Hark, the Herald Angels Sing*), and then damn 'un?'

Moonta carol-singing was heard at its best at the concerts held on Christmas night each year at the rotunda in Victoria Park. These concerts......continued without a break for more than thirty years. The area was lit by Chinese lanterns suspended from trees, and a big crowd listened to a two-hour programme by the combined choirs of the district. The singing was of the hearty kind favoured by Cornish folk – 'Like 'ee used to be,' one old-timer said, 'before they music singers spoilt singin'.'

When the mines closed down and there was a dispersal of population, the concerts were abandoned, but the carols did not die. Cornish folk are like the nightingale; they sing because they must.

At home as well as in Australia.

CHRISTMAS CHEER

William Bottrell, perhaps the finest of the early Cornish folklorists offered this recipe for mead, a favourite tipple to quench the Christmas thirst, in the 1870s:

> The old method of making mead, or metheglin, in West Cornwall was to put four pounds of honey to one gallon of water; boil it one hour, skim it well, then add one ounce of hops to every gallon, and boil it half-an-hour longer, and let it stand till next day. Put it into your cask or bottles. To every gallon add a gill of brandy; stop it lightly till the fermentation is over; then stop it very loose. Keep it one year before you tap. More recently the old ladies who were noted for making good mead (or sweet-drink as they call it), boiled the combs from which the honey had been drained until all the honey that remained was extracted. They then strained it, and added as much more honey as made the drink strong enough to float an egg. To every gallon they added one ounce of cloves; the same of all-spice; half-an-ounce of coriander; the same weight of caraway-seed. Sometimes, cinnamon and mace were used instead of the seeds. Others, who preferred the flavour and perfume of aromatic plants, boiled in the water, before they added the honey, the tops of the sweet-briar, flowers of thyme, rosemary, sweet marjoram, or any other sweet herbs they liked; then finished as above.

Punchbowl & Ladle, Penelewey.

Something less exotic than mead was, perhaps, responsible for the actions behind this report from the *West Briton* for Boxing Day 1851:

> On Saturday night last, John Charles Pascoe, labourer, and Bawden Wills were drinking together in the Swan public-house, Kenwyn Street, Truro. Between ten and eleven o'clock, Wills being too drunk to walk home, Pascoe agreed to carry him on his back to his house in Castle-street. Pascoe took him up, but on leaving the house hitched his toe against the curb, and both fell to the ground together. Pascoe, on getting up, laid hold of a man called Clarke, and accused him of tripping him up; a scuffle then took place between them, and Clarke threw Pascoe and broke his arm. Dr Bullimore being applied to, directed Pascoe to be immediately taken to the Infirmary, where he now remains under surgical care.

The Swan was described as 'well-accustomed' in 1801 but, considering the quality of its future customers, it is hardly surprising that it was demolished in 1899. The Punchbowl & Ladle at Penelewey, though, still flourishes, partly due to its proximity to Tony Shaw's cottage. Tony recorded the following narrative verbatim from another regular customer, Reg Green; it recalls an incident of only a few years ago:

> The week before Christmas, a few of the local men turned up at the Punchbowl for their lunchtime pint only to find that the pub was closed. After banging on the door, one of the men looked through the window and saw the new landlord (who had recently retired from the Navy) sitting in front of a blazing fire and getting slowly drunk. Deciding that drastic action had to be taken, as there was no response to their continued hammering, Jack climbed onto the roof and covered the smoking chimney with a piece of slate. The others watched as the room filled with smoke and, as this slowly penetrated the landlord's drunken stupor, he stumbled to his feet and opened the door, allowing the locals to rush in. Jack removed the slate from the chimney and joined his friends at the bar demanding their pints, which the landlord begrudgingly served.

The *West Briton* included this story from Bodmin police on 18 January 1861:

> On Monday John Williams was charged with having been drunk on the 28th December last. The prisoner, who is in the receipt of 2s6d (12½p) per week as a pauper, had been drinking, or as he stated, on the 'ran-tan' at Christmas, and getting very drunk, was obliged to be taken home in a wheel-barrow, though he said it was owing to the state of the roads, being so slippery that he could not walk. On

getting home he became very abusive, and annoyed his neighbours so much that the constable was obliged to be called in and remain with him all night.

While nineteenth-century excuses seem to have been no less flimsy that today's, the use of the term 'ran-tan' is interesting: it is now far more common in Australia than in Britain, perhaps emigrating with the Cornish miners. Its replacement is 'binge drinking', a modern phenomenon according to the gutter press: not so, as this report from Helston, printed in the *West Briton* for 31 December 1874 proves:

A little after eleven o'clock on Christmas-day a lot of noisy fellows were turned out of a public-house, and having provided themselves with a supply of beer in a jar they camped in the centre of the principal street in the town; there they remained drinking, dancing, and shouting, interspersing these proceedings by shrieking carols and (profane) melodies. Between 11.30 and midnight a resident in the lower part of the street was quietly going in the direction of his house, when he was recognised and saluted with yells and menaces, so that he had to retrace his steps. Soon after this PC Wedlock, who had previously dislodged the party, appeared, and for the time dispersed them, but shortly after four of them again commenced the disturbances, and after some threats, in which these affairs end at Helston, the householders of the locality were allowed to retire to rest in comparative quiet. While these drunken fellows were thus disporting themselves, a few yards off two girls were observed to go and smash the window of a private house. Fortunately for the occupant, the girls were seen and the damage was made good on the following morning.

Q, in his short story *My Grandfather, Hendry Watty*, describes his characters spending 'the fore-part of the evening over the eggy-hot', while Margaret Courtney recalls a Christmas Eve supper where 'egg-hot, or eggy-hot, was the principal drink'. The recipe for eggy'ot (with the emphasis on the last syllable) is simple: two eggs beaten with two tablespoons of sugar, then one quart of hot beer is poured over the top and stirred briskly. Courtney suggests rum as an additional ingredient, with the mixture poured from one jug to another until it became white and covered with froth.

Mrs John Bonham, of whom little is known, published two 'long' short stories under the title *Christmas in Cornwall 60 Years Ago* in 1898. Both were set in the fictional village of St Cadge, based very closely on Cadgwith Cove on the Lizard peninsula. We will be meeting more of Mrs Bonham's characters later in this book but, for now, here is her humorous recollection of eggy-hot, confirming Courtney's method of making it:

> The old man lived alone and 'did' for himself; and his two rooms were a credit to him. He was very fond of his nieces, especially liking to hear them sing. So on this Christmas Eve he called, asking them to come over and have some 'eggy hot' with him, the usual drink at that season.
>
> 'Iss, uncle,' said Mary Jane, quite pleased with the prospect; 'we'll come arver an' maake the eggy hot, an' sing to 'a bit afterwards.'
>
> 'No, no,' he replied quickly. 'I'll git'n all ready 'gen you come. I can maake eggy hot s'well as any womon I knaw, you see ef I caan't.'
>
> At eight o'clock the two girls stepped across the village to their uncle's little cottage. There was no blind to the kitchen window, so they peeped in to see how the preparations were going on. There sat the old man at the table with a quart basin before him, eating

Christmas cheer. (From a drawing by R. Goldcroft)

something out of it with a spoon. Wondering to see him taking broth on such an evening, they watched him with much curiosity, and soon discovered that it was the eggy hot he was devouring with all haste. They could plainly see the great lumps of egg in the spoon as he raised it to his mouth.

'Poor uncle,' cried Mary Jane, convulsed with laughter. 'Why, aw ben maakin' the eggy hot, an' aw den't knaw how to thraw et foorth an' back, an' the eggs es all gone in great lumps.'

'Sarve'm right,' said Sarah Ann, decisively. 'I wanted for 'n to lev es maake et, but aw do alles think aw can do so well as any womon. Hallo, uncle!' she cried, bursting into the room, 'what are 'a eaten' of 'on?'

'Why, I was 'aven' a bit of somefen' 'fore you come. Now, my dears, lev us be gone an' maake the eggy hot far our lives.'

The girls had not the heart to let out the secret. All three set to work, and soon a large brown jug was filled with the smoking

> beverage. And they sat around the Christmas logs in the old open chimney, and the girls sang the old-fashioned carols, much to uncle's delight. Evidently he was not grieving over the loss of the beer, eggs, and sugar that had turned out such a miserable failure.

There is a story from the Ring o' Bells pub in St Issey, near Padstow, that smacks of urban myth but, of course, is allegedly true. In early May 'not long ago', a local lad had over-indulged at Padstow's famous Obby Oss festival and fallen asleep in the pub. While he was unconscious, the landlord and a group of pub regulars decorated the bar with Christmas finery and he awoke to the singing of rousing carols. After a time, he was convinced that he had 'lost' seven months of his life. At the annual 'Second of May' singaround in the pub today – and this is definitely true – the company always give a spirited rendition of *While Shepherds Watched*, to the beautiful local tune Lyngham.

To conclude this section, here is another example of Christmas cheer in the twentieth century. Tony Deane wrote this piece some years ago, as part of a longer essay; it has not previously been published:

> By the late 1960s, the breathalyser had failed to make much of an impact in the remoter areas of Cornwall. I was spending Christmas in Gorran, as guest of a former legendary landlady of the Barley Sheaf Inn, while spending much time and money with the then-current legendary landlord.
>
> After a heavy Christmas Eve, I awoke to a perfect Cornish Christmas Day: a light covering of snow reflecting a gleaming blue sky. Time for a medicinal stroll before breakfast, I thought. Leaving my digs, I walked uphill past Gorran school – temporary buildings then, after Anne Treneer's 'Schoolhouse in the Wind' had burnt down – and right into Crooked Lane, aptly-named and, dating from the Iron Age, perhaps the oldest road in the parish. While

completing the circle back into Gorran, passing the Barley Sheaf on the way, I wondered at the regular dents in the hedgerows: surely they were not there yesterday.

Over breakfast, I asked my hostess if she could explain these phenomena. She had no problem. Obviously, she said, several celebrants had left the Barley rather the worse for wear on Christmas Eve and their cars just would not do as asked.

By the following day the dents were beginning to heal.

SCHOOLHOUSE IN THE WIND

By Anne Treneer

Anne Treneer (1891-1966) was the youngest child of Gorran Board School's first headmaster, appointed in 1877 by Revd C.R. Sowell, the local vicar for thirty-four years. She followed four boys, including Wilfred – Cap'n in this extract – and Maurice, who moved to America and invented Alka-Seltzer, and one girl, Susan. Although Anne's career in teaching took her away from home for many years, she remained devoted to Cornwall and was elected a Bard of the Cornish Gorsedd in 1945, taking the name *Flogh Plu Woran*, Child of Gorran. She returned home in 1956, when she retired to live with her sister in Gerrans, just a few miles west of her native parish. She was well-regarded as a poet and wrote several academic studies, including *The Sea in English Literature*, plus biographies of the Arabian scholar Charles M. Doughty and Sir Humphrey Davy, perhaps Cornwall's most famous son: The *Mercurial Chemist* remains a standard text to this day. Her most popular works, though, form a trilogy of reminiscences: the first, *Schoolhouse in the Wind*, published in 1944, concerns her early life in Gorran and neighbouring St Michael Caerhays and depicts a vibrant childhood in pre-tourism Cornwall, including this delightful portrait of Christmas. The school, designed by the prolific Silvanus Trevail remained 'in the wind' until its destruction by fire in 1967, just a year after Anne Treneer's death.

> I can remember when time was not measured at all; when it lay like an uncharted ocean about me. In the midst of this immersion I can hear a joint conclave of boys' voices with a murmur from Susan: Christmas will soon be here. This Christmas shone as something immanent and splendid. I suppose actually it is not that first sudden Christmas I can remember, but all the early Christmases at Gorran united in one chain. The boys would write my notes to Santa Claus and set them afire. If, after the paper had caught and flamed and dulled and shrivelled and turned grey it flew, light as a ghost, up the chimney, I should get what I wanted.
>
> Mother made the Christmas puddings, with children round, tasting this and that, and all of us having a stir. There would be a wonderful smell of cooking and baking in the house, loaves of saffron cake full of lemon peel and currants, a great ham boiled and a tongue to go with it. The goose would have arrived from Tregerrick. For a week or two beforehand Christmas extras would appear in Agnes' shop to tempt our pennies from us, especially we invested in coloured baubles for the tree, silver trinkets and sugar animals. I remember in particular a pink sugar mouse which I bought, and a wonderful little bell which was Cap'n's and which tinkled on the tree. There was a silver star which went on the top each year, and each year we had tiny coloured candles in little candlesticks, altogether smaller and more fairy-like than the candles on trees nowadays.
>
> The tree always came from Cotna. On Christmas Eve we would take the wheelbarrow and be off to Cotna where our friends the Kendals lived. We brought home laurel and fir; box, bay and holly; trails of ivy from tree trunks, and rich ivy berries. Somebody carried

the Christmas tree. It all seemed festive, even Shot who went with us would be spryer than usual and feel an extra stirring in his tail. We decorated the whole of the downstairs of the house; hung mistletoe over each doorway, and then we set up the tree in the dining-room and hung it with our treasures. The tree was never in the parlour; that was kept fresh and clean for Christmas Day. Christmas Eve was in the dining-room because, before the lighting of the tree, would come supper, for which even I stayed up.

A fire of wood and coal would be blazing, for we had our own wood-pile at the back behind the trap-house, where we sawed up our own Christmas fire with a cross-cut saw. I often sat on the tree trunk to keep it steady on the 'horse'. The red curtains would be drawn; the lamp lit; the table set. No room cosier than ours on a winter night. The ham and the tongue, as yet uncut, were placed before my mother who always carved. She sat at the head of the table; my father at the foot; I next him, Susan next my mother; the boys two on either side of the table between us. With anticipatory glee we watched my mother make a preliminary incision into the ham and cut the first slice, pink and white, thin and curling. There is no such ham nowadays; it was cured with sugar according to a recipe of Granny Nott's. The tongue matched it. We feasted. Apples and nuts followed and drinks. My father loved wine but could rarely afford it; as a rule he was content with a little barrel of beer on tap. But at Christmas time two little bottles always arrived, a bottle of port for my father, and a bottle of something for my mother. My father had the temperament to be cherished by the grape. He should have had wine oftener. I can see him now, his blue eyes sparkling at the rare indulgence. We children had something home-made, blackberry or sloe. My mother's favourite drink was a little whisky or gin. She never cared for wine of any kind, whereas a stray bottle of claret or sherry would rejoice my father's blood.

After supper was over and the table cleared the great moment of Christmas arrived for me. We let the fire die down a little, put out the lamp, and lit the candles on the tree. I cannot account for the intense pleasure these tiny points of light gave me as they lit up the dark tree, the shining baubles, the silver star at the top, and Cap'n's little bell. There were no gifts. We did not tie presents to the tree nor place them at the foot. The tree was simply for beauty. We let the candles burn half way down and then snuffed them. The second lighting would be on Christmas night.

In the dining-room was a small organ. The lamp was now relit, and candles for my father to see the music. We gathered round and sang such things as, 'It came upon a midnight clear', 'Stars all bright are beaming', 'When the winter's sun was set', and 'There came three Ships'. My brothers had good voices; so had Susan and my mother. My father sang bass. I had an ear, and early knew the words and tunes so well that I have never forgotten them. But I had nothing to sing with. My notes like the house-martin's were inward.

After the singing, Susan and Cap'n and I went to bed to hang our stockings up. The elder boys sat up till later. But in what seemed to us the dead vast and middle of the night – actually, I am told it was late in the evening, before my parents had left the fireside – the carol singers came. Sometimes the ringers came, too, with handbells. My mother would come in with a candle to wake us. By its flickering light, sitting up in bed in the long-sleeved white nightdresses trimmed with embroidery which we wore both winter and summer, we would listen. I cannot describe the fascination of this music. The ringers would ring a carillon on the handbells and play a carol on them. Then the carol party would sing 'While shepherds watched their flocks by night', 'O come, all ye faithful', 'Angel hosts in bright array', 'Hark, the herald', and 'Christians awake'. Confused with sleep and with the lovely story of the shepherds and the baby of which

I never wearied, it seemed to me that everything was happening at that moment. The shepherds were on the Greeb, the baby was in a nest of Trevesan hay, and in our sky was the great light with the angels singing, 'Glory to God in the highest, and on earth peace, good will towards men'.

So far our stockings would still be hanging limp from the wooden foot of our bed, but magically when we woke in the morning they were bulging. Parcels too big to go into the stockings were ranged near; we would seize our booty and go into the boys' room. The stockings were all filled alike – nuts in the toe, then an orange, a packet of dates, a packet of broad figs, and a packet of sweets. The sweets were of mixed kinds, some noble, some common. With these we played swaps – a superior sweet being swapped for two or even three of a plebeian variety. The formula went: 'Swap, sir?' 'Yes, sir.' 'How many, sir?' 'Three, sir.' 'No, sir.' 'Two, sir.' 'Yes, sir.' – or according to the bidding. This was a great game. The hazel nuts we cracked with our teeth; but pasty nuts (brazils) had to wait for the crackers, though I can remember Cap'n cracking his in the hinge of the door. The scene must have been of the wildest confusion. I would pop into Howard's bed, Susan into Maurice's, and we would undo our parcels. One of the best presents I remember was a picture book which on each page had a kind of thick paper pulley at the bottom. One pulled this flap and the picture changed – a harvest field with corn-wagons and harvesters would become a Christmas scene with snowflakes falling on a woodcutter and his dog; three horses in a stall would change to a sow with piglets and a goose with goslings in a farmyard. There were more of these changing pictures. Another gift I especially remember is a humming top, and another a Noah's Ark with all kinds of animals. We would go out to show our parents the presents. I believed implicitly in Santa Claus when I was very little, but after a year or two the rumour reached even me that once upon a time Cap'n had heard my father drop a heavy copy of the *Arabian Nights* on his stockinged toe, and betray himself as all too human.

Christmas Day was joyful, but not holy and enchanted as Christmas Eve was. We went to church in the morning – Maurice and Howard with my father to Caerhays, and the rest of us with my mother to Gorran. All the other children were in the choir, but I never attained to this honour. I sat with my mother about six rows back from the pulpit, and in sermon time snuggled against her sealskin jacket (an old sealskin bequeathed her by my richer Aunt Sarah). I sang my best and was proud of being able to find all the places in the prayer book. Hymn tunes carry with them extraordinarily strong powers of association. 'Sing ye the songs of praise' or Mrs Alexander's 'Once in royal David's city', with which Mr Sowel began the Christmas Day service because it was a favourite with my mother, fills me with nostalgia; it brings back Gorran Church in every detail, to the ivy wound round the slender poles which supported the oil-lamps. We did not then know the loveliest of the medieval carols which later my brother Howard was to help to popularize. By the time that we sang at home – 'The Holly and the Ivy'; 'Lulla, lulla, Thou little tiny child'; 'Down in yon forest'; 'Green grow'th the holly'; 'As Joseph was a-walking'; 'The first good joy that Mary had'; 'Joseph dearest, Joseph mine'; 'Torches, torches, run with torches' – I was too old to feel quite that ecstatic pleasure I should have taken in them when I was six or seven. Some of the great hymns we had of course. My father would sing out 'O come, all ye faithful', which, I can hear him saying, was magnificent; whereas he was scornful of Mr Sowel's choice of carols. He would imitate the old parson's bass notes in 'Carol, sweetly carol', and say that 'Like silver lamps in a distant shrine' was nothing but tinsel. But I think I connected the silver lamps with our candles on the tree, and I loved them. I loved another equally despised Christmas hymn beginning 'Last night I laid me down to sleep'.

I cannot remember Christmas Day dinner nearly as vividly as I remember Christmas Eve supper. I think when it came to the point I did not much like goose. In later years a couple of fowls were substituted for it; we never ran to turkey until I was nearly grown up. The pudding was chiefly valued by me because of the threepenny piece one might have with luck in one's helping. Otherwise I liked the almonds and raisins and sultanas and peel which were among its ingredients much better raw than cooked.

The best part of Christmas Day was the walk to Gruda with my father after the late midday dinner, and the coming in after it to tea in the parlour. Tea was in the parlour on Christmas Days. Commonly when my mother had tea in the parlour with a friend the children had it together in the kitchen – there were three doors, a passage and a room between. There is a story that once when mother was wielding her best silver teapot and enjoying Mrs Kendal's company the door was suddenly burst open and a very dirty Cap'n appeared saying, 'Mother, Howard's got tart; why can't I have tart? I want tart.' But on Christmas Day we were all exalted to the best room for tea, and it was a tea after our heart's desire. We did not stay up to supper on Christmas night. Our parents must have been glad to get rid of us. After tea we played games and sang, and ate almonds and muscatels and roasted chestnuts. Then we went into the dark dining-room and, for the second time, lit the candles on our tree. But the glory had departed; it was never quite the same the second night. We let the candles burn right down, and the splendour of Christmas was over. Though the decorations remained up, and the tree was left standing till Twelfth Night, all had grown ordinary.

On our Christmas cards would be pictures of snow, robins and holly; but we never had actual snow for any Christmas I can remember as a small child. At Caerhays I can remember a snowy Christmas. At Gorran we longed for it but did not get it. More often the weather was curiously mild. The birds of calm brooded over two little girls sitting in their nightdresses listening entranced to the celestial music.

THE SEVEN JOYS OF MARY

This carol is not unique to Cornwall but many versions of it, including the one below, have been collected there. In this format it probably dates from the fifteenth century but later versions, perhaps from the eighteenth century, include twelve joys and offer a precursor to the much later *Twelve Days of Christmas*. In his study *The English Carol* (1958), Erik Routley suggests that the song strays 'almost into the realm of nursery rhyme': a particularly astute comment as it shares a tune with *The Old Grey Duck*, a song popular among Cornish children.

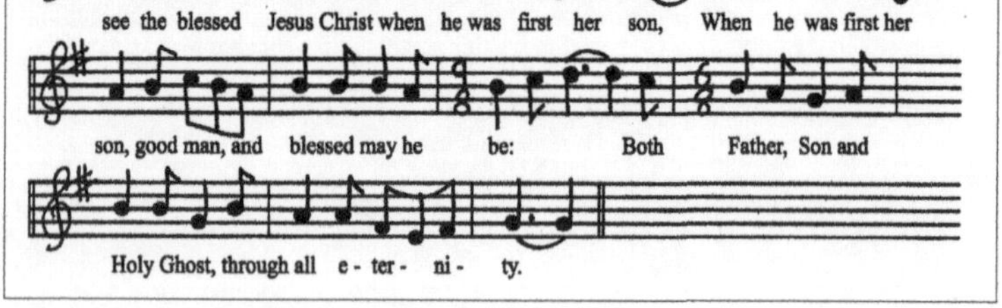

The first good joy that Mary had it was the joy of one:
To see the blessed Jesus Christ when he was first her son,
When he was first her son, good man, and blessed may he be:
Both Father, Son and Holy Ghost through all eternity.

The next good joy that Mary had it was the joy of two:
To see her own son Jesus Christ to make the lame to go,
To make the lame to go, etc.

The next good joy that Mary had it was the joy of three:
To see her own Jesus Christ to make the blind to see,
To make the blind to see, etc.

The next good joy that Mary had it was the joy of four:
To see her own son Jesus Christ to read the Bible o'er,
To read the Bible o'er, etc.

The next good joy that Mary had it was the joy of five:
To see her own son Jesus Christ to bring the dead alive,
To bring the dead alive, etc.

The next good joy that Mary had it was the joy of six:
To see her own son Jesus Christ upon the crucifix,
Upon the crucifix, etc.

And the last good joy that Mary had it was the joy of seven:
To see her own son Jesus Christ to wear the crown of Heaven,
To wear the crown of Heaven, etc.

OF MUMMERS AND GUISERS

Guising – or, in Cornwall, goose- or geese-dancing – is one of the oldest 'turn of the year' traditions. It occurs in many forms but always involves disguise: hence the term 'guising' itself. Sometimes local custom demands the use of animal skins or masks but the most basic method of concealing one's identity is by the application of burnt cork, charcoal or soot, if the guiser is white, or whitewash, if black.

In our *Folklore of Cornwall*, published in 2003, we described Padstow's Mummers' Days (know as 'Darkie Days' before 2005), which take place on Boxing Day and New Year's Day each year. Then, the local musicians, known as The Merrymakers, most of whom also participate in the annual May Day Obby Oss festival, parade through the town, playing and singing songs from nineteenth-century minstrel shows, such as *Poor Old Joe, Old Mother Flipper-Flopper* and *Bungananary*. The shows were very popular and the songs caught on in the more remote areas, to become regarded as local folksongs: Padstow is only one such area and similar traditions survive in the north-east and in parts of East Anglia. The 'blacking-up' element is likely to be a throwback to guising as there is a belief in Padstow that to daub a spectator with black is to guarantee good luck for the coming year.

There is an alternative theory to the origins of Mummers' Days, suggesting that slave ships allowed their human cargoes to exercise on the harbour, where they sang the songs later picked up by the local population. As the songs mostly date from around the middle of the nineteenth century, we believe this is unlikely but it helped to fuel the controversy that now surrounds the ceremony

Mummers' Days were not always restricted to Padstow: here is an extract from Philip Marsden's moving novel *The Main Cages* (2002), set in the fictional West Cornwall village of Penmayne in 1934:

> On Boxing Day Whaler Cuffe banged his stick on the floor and announced he had been cooped for too long inside. 'I would like to go carousing.' Jack took him to see Benny Stone and they drank brandy and then some others came and they went to the Fountain Inn and Whaler told some improbable stories and the crew of the *Constantine* applauded even though they knew they were supposed to be sceptical about 'Whaler's fabling'.
>
> Polmayne shook itself down that Christmas. The children sooted their faces and went Darkey Partyin'. Jack and Whaler set off for the dance in the Freeman Reading Rooms. They carried on somewhere else and it was almost dawn when they staggered home along the front. Eliza Tucker was sweeping ths steps of her store, and stopped to watch them: 'The blind drunk leading the blind!' They were still tipsy at lunchtime and Mrs Cuffe refused to feed them. So they went out again. That afternoon the Town Band left the Fountain Inn for Porth but they took a short cut and the flautist dropped his flute in a stream; the percussionists were found by Ivor Dawkins next morning, sleeping in one of Crowdy's barns.

Then, from Newlyn, perhaps the model for Polmayne, Charles Lee – a London journalist who settled in and wrote superbly about Cornwall – reported in his journal entry for 15 December 1892:

> At Christmas, I am told, boys and men go about the village in disguise, dancing and singing in the houses. They are called 'guise-dancers', with guise pronounced as in French.

Robert Hunt, with Bottrell, the finest of researchers into Cornish folklore, was born in Plymouth in 1807. He trained in science and medicine in London, where he studied the chemistry of photography. After a period in Falmouth from 1840, he was appointed Keeper of Mining Records at the Government School of Mines in London, where he spent the remainder of his professional career. He published *Popular Romances of the West of England* in 1881, six years before his death. His seminal book did not ignore guising.

> Of late years, at this season, in the Islands of Scilly, the young people exercise a sort of gallantry called 'goose-dancing'. The maidens are dressed up for young men, and the young men for maidens; and thus disguised, they visit their neighbours in companies, where they dance and make jokes upon what has happened in the island, and every one is humorously 'told their own', without offence being taken. By this sort of sport, according to yearly custom and toleration, there is a spirit of wit and drollery kept up among the people. The music and dancing done, they are treated with liquor, and then they go to the next house of entertainment.

This piece is quoted from the antiquarian Joseph Strutt, writing in 1801, but Hunt added:

> This custom was by no means confined to the Islands of Scilly. In nearly every town and large village in Cornwall, geese-dancing, – not goose-dancing, - formed one of the Christmas entertainments. The term was applied to the old Christmas plays, and indeed to any kind of sport in which characters were assumed by the performers, or disguises worn.

He then quoted, from the not entirely accurate *Table Book*, that guise-dancing:

> ... has found a last retreat at St Ives, - this is the only town in the country where the old Cornish Christmas revelry is kept up with spirit. The guise-dancing time is the twelve nights after Christmas, i.e., from Christmas-day to Twelfth-day. Guise-dancing at St Ives is no more nor less than a pantomimic representation or bal masque on an extensive scale, the performers outnumbering the audience.

Even more disparaging was the *St Ives Correspondent* for 1861, again cited by Hunt:

> On the whole the guise-dancing has degenerated very much this last twenty years. It was formerly the custom for parties to get up a little play, and go from house to house to recite their droll oddities, and levy contributions on their hearers in the form of cake or plum-pudding. Old Father Christmas and bold King George were favourite characters. It is not uncommon to see a most odiously-disguised person with a bedroom utensil, asking the blushing bystanders if there is 'any need of me'. Some of the dresses are, indeed, very smart, and even costly; but for the most part they consist of old clothes, arranged in the oddest manner, even frightfully ugly.

A.K. Hamilton Jenkin, writing in 1934, was more well-disposed towards the old custom:

> The period between Christmas Day and Twelfth Night (the latter still kept by Cornish miners in 1760 as 'Old Christmas Day') has from time immemorial been devoted to Guise Dancing. During this cold and wintry season of the year the streets of St Ives and Penzance are still nightly invaded by bands of young people attired in strange and grotesque costume. In almost every case the boys are dressed as girls and the girls as boys, some of them cleverly representing historical or local characters, others merely disguised with blackened faces and Nottingham lace veils – but all enjoying themselves as much as if they were frolicking beneath a midsummer sky. If the night is fine, parties will often group themselves together at the street corners, where an impromptu dance takes place, to the accompaniment of drums, mouth organs, and concertinas. The police, meanwhile, look on benignly, for guise dancing is recognised by law no less than custom, and little rowdyism ever mars the proceedings during the fortnight in which they are now officially permitted.

The ubiquitous Margaret Courtney, from 1890, was more forthright:

> From Christmas to Twelfth-tide parties of mummers known as 'Goose or Geese-dancers' paraded the streets in all sorts of disguises, with masks on. They often behaved in such an unruly manner that women and children were afraid to venture out. If the doors of the houses were not locked they would enter uninvited and stay, playing all kinds of antics, until money was given them to go away.

She quoted from *The Land's End District*, written by R. Edmunds in 1862:

> A well-known character amongst them, about fifty years ago (c1810), was the hobby-horse, represented by a man carrying a piece of wood in the form of a horse's head and neck, with some contrivance for opening and shutting the mouth with a loud snapping noise, the performer being so covered with horse-cloth or hide of a horse as to resemble the animal, whose curvetings, biting and other motions he imitated. Some of these 'guise-dancers' occasionally masked themselves with the skins of the head of bullocks having the horns on.

A popular Christmas 'guising' play was *Duffy and the Devil*, often associated with the Lovell family of much-haunted Trewoofe, near Lamorna. Ignoring *Rumpelstiltskin*, Courtney comments, after Bottrell, that:

> It turns upon the legend, common in all countries, of a woman who had sold herself to a devil, who was to do her knitting or spinning for her. He was to claim his bargain at the end of three years if she could find out his name before the time expired. Of course, she gets it by stratagem; her husband, who knows nothing of the compact, first meets the devil, whilst out hunting, the day before the time is up, and makes him half-drunk. An old woman in Duffy's pay (Witch Bet) completes the work, and in that state the devil sings the following words, ending with his name, which Bet remembers and tells her mistress:-
>
> I've knit and spun for her
> Three years to the day;
> To-morrow she shall ride with me
> Over land and over sea.
> Far away! far away!
> For she can never know
> That my name is 'Tarraway'.

Bet and some other witches then sing in chorus:-

By night and by day
We will dance and play
With our noble captain,
Tarraway! Tarraway!

Robert Hunt has a variation of the play, where the devil sings:

Duffy my lady, you'll never know – what?
That my name is Ferry-top, Ferry-top – top.

Miss Courtney concludes her description of guising with a sober paragraph:

> These 'goose-dancers' became such a terror to the respectable inhabitants of Penzance that the Corporation put them down about ten years since (c1880), and every Christmas-eve a notice is posted in conspicuous places forbidding their appearance in the streets, but they still perambulate the streets of St Ives. Guise-dancing wit must have very much deteriorated since the beginning of the [nineteenth] century, as writers before that time speak of the mirth it afforded; and the saying, 'as good as a Christmas-play', is commonly used to describe a very witty or funny thing.

The recollections of William Paynter, dating back to the 1830s, were published by his daughter Winifred in 1927, under the title *Old St Ives*. Guising, of course, featured in his memories:

> The time between Christmas Day and Twelfth Night has for many years been sacred to Guise Dancing. Formerly the Mummers used to act plays, 'St George and the Dragon' being the favourite, but this

had died out in St Ives in my young days. At that time people used to go in fancy dress to various houses, and attempt to conceal their identity by speaking in an assumed voice. They were well received, caused great amusement, and were regaled with food and drink before going on somewhere else. Gradually an element of rowdyism crept in. Trusting to their disguise the guise dancers were often noisy and abjectionable, and finally their visits were discountenanced. It then became the custom for them to parade the streets. A blackened face, a false nose, a window curtain draped across the shoulders passed as 'dressing up' and provided an excuse for shouting and screaming, so that, in latter years, the general feeling has been that the sooner guise dancing came to an end the better. It was however properly organised by a committee in 1927, when over two hundred took part in it, and a very effective pageant was the result.

The horrors of a committee never troubled Mrs Bonham: this, from her *Christmas in Cornwall 60 Years Ago*, published in 1898; please ignore the inconsistent dialect.

The Collinses were singing the last carol when the maid came into the room, and whispered to her mistress, who turned to her husband and said a few words. The young people, observing all this, were longing to know what was going on. Scarcely had the last note died away when Mary Jane asked eagerly, 'Wha's the matter 'on, mawther?'

'Why the Christmas play es out theere; want to come In bit.'

'Aw, mother,' cried all the children together, 'lev thom come in, iss mawther do.'

'But they'll kick up such a ranty-mis-skit (uproar),' said she.

'Never mind for wance,' replied her husband, 'the roouds es dry as boones, so they waan't dirty the floor.'

'Well thon,' said his wife, 'tell thom to come in,' and Cherry disappeared, delighted to carry out the command.

After some shuffling outside the door in walks a masked figure with a nose! – out of all proportion to the rest of his face. This striking personage is attired in a black coat, gaily adorned with bits of red cloth sewn here and there. Short pieces of straw threaded like beads, intermixed with tiny circles of red cloth, hang from different parts of his body. His head is adorned with an immense paper hat in the gayest of colours, with cock's feathers tuck in to add to the effect. After making a few turns up and down the room, in a feigned voice he introduces himself as follows:-

Here come I, old Father Christmas,
Welcome or welcome not,
I hope old Father Christmas
Will never be forgot.
With a head like a pig
And a body like a sow
And a great long nose
Like the beam of a plough.

This speech being finished, two more figures, also gaily dressed and masked, enter. All talk together, till the new-comers quarrel and commence to fight with swords (blunt ones of course). The skirmish comes to a sudden end by one of them falling on the floor. The conqueror looks around and asks in a tone of distress ...

Es other doctor to be found,
To cure this deep and deadly wound?

... 'wound' rhyming with 'found'. In an instant he who personates the doctor, and who has been waiting outside, springs in holding a black bottle, but, instead of going to his patient at once, he gives to the audience an account of the various ills he professes to cure, and all the while the figure on the floor lies stretched at full length without any sign of life. Then stooping over him the doctor puts the bottle to his lips and shouts, 'Rise, and fight King George again.'

Up jumps the wounded man, suddenly cured, and he and his former enemy go at it once more. But after a while the fighting turns to dancing, turning, jumping, and other movements in which join Father Christmas, doctor, and other figures in masks. At last a hat is passed round and the Collinses feel in their pockets, and out come pence, which are willingly given, all being delighted with the performance.

Mrs Collins brings in some saffron cake, which the poor creatures cannot eat because of their masks; so they take it away with them. The family then begin to guess who the performers are. – some having rather betrayed themselves by not carefully feigning their voices.

Mr Collins and his brother have thoroughly enjoyed it all. They have been accustomed every Christmas since their boyhood to see the old play acted. For several nights this is repeated in the neighbouring farmhouses and cottages, till by the time the festive season is over, the pence which the performers have collected amount to quite a respectable sum.

Q's grandfather, Dr Jonathan Couch, born in 1789, was probably Polperro's most gifted son. He was a naturalist and ichthyologist, skills he combined with his career as a physician when he returned to Polperro from London medical schools in 1810. His most important publication was, perhaps, *Fishes of the British Isles* (1862), still regarded as a seminal work, but here we are indebted to *The History of Polperro*: published in 1871, shortly after his death, Couch offers a vibrant account of a Cornish Christmas, including the mummers' play:

> Christmas … a time of genial mirth and heartiness, when general social regulations are by common consent relaxed. Misrule has happily gone out, and is replaced by soberer, but still noisy jollity. The time is notified by the evergreens with which every window is garnished. Poor old women now 'go a gooding', travelling the parish over to collect from their richer neighbours the measure of flour for the cake, made yellow with saffron and besprinkled with currants; or the Christmas pudding. On Christmas-eve the mirth begins, when the *mock* or yule-log is lighted, it may be, from a portion saved from the last year's fire. In farmhouses the husbandmen and neighbours come in about evening and spend some hours in singing carols, clearing their voices by occasional draughts of cider. The travelling hawker has been round with his penny broadsheet, where 'The first good joy our Mary had', 'As I sat on a sunny bank' and 'God rest ye merry gentlemen' are in company with 'As shepherds watched their flocks by night', Kirke White's 'Star of Bethlehem' and others which seem out of place in such almost ludicrous company. The provincial Catnach has illustrated the sheet at the top by the 'Flight into Egypt' and other similar scenes.
>
> In town the family, flocking round the *mock*, are interrupted by the cheerfully tolerated intrusion of the goosey-dancers. The boys and girls rifle their parents' wardrobes of old gowns and coats, and disguise themselves, their mien, and speech, so cleverly that it is impossible to identify them. They are allowed, and are not slow to take, the large amount of licence which the season warrants; for it is considered a mark of a churlish disposition to take offence at anything they do or say. Accordingly they enter without ceremony;

dance, sing and carry on an extemporaneous dialogue well spiced with native wit. After testing, unasked perhaps, whatever may be on the table, they beg money to make merry with. The children are much amused, and the mummers leave with a benediction.

''Twas as good as a Christmas play', is still our best comparison for anything that is funny, though this entertainment has for nearly half a century been discontinued. It may have been a remnant of the *guary-mirkl*, or miracle play, which in remote times was performed in the round or amphitheatre to amuse our Celtic forefathers; the latter dramas however have not been like the earlier ones, on Scripture subjects, but based on later romance. The last one I have intelligence of represented the achievements of George, and his victory over the Dragon. The theatre was a long room over some fish-cellar, or the largest chamber of the inn, and the players were the boys and girls of the town. A subscription had been previously made for the purchase of 'properties', and the services of the damsels had been volunteered in arranging the costumes and other adornments. The play opened with the entrance of a page, who, after a brief speech, introduced a white-haired, tottering old man, yet having a mirthful eye and a ruddy face, who announced himself thus:

Here come I, old Father Christmas,
Welcome, or welcome not,
I hope old Father Christmas
Will never be forgot.

After improvising some fun, he went out, to be followed by the Turkish knight, breathing loud words of defiance against St George. The armed saint suddenly appeared upon the stage and recounted his exploits:

... with my sword and spear
I won three crowns of gold.
I fought the dragon bold
And brought him to the slaughter,
By that I gained fair Sabra,
The King of Egypt's daughter.

They fought and the Turkish knight fell. St George, with the humanity which should accompany bravery, called for a doctor to heal this 'deep and deadly wound'. A doctor came, and by the aid of a little 'Elicumpane' raised the Turkish Knight for a time but only to fall finally before the onslaught of St George. A hobby-horse trotted in and removed the dead body. A bold dragon who had infested the country was next defied by the Saint, who was not daunted by the entrance of the dreadful monster, although he threatened,

With my long teeth and scurvy jaw
I'll seize thee up within my maw.

The dragon was then valiantly encountered by the knight, and after some struggles, slain. This part of the dragon was not played without some danger, for, it being necessary that he breathe forth sulphurous flames, accomplished by putting a squib in his snout, the explosive compound was sometimes thrown inward by the incautious elevation of the monstrous snout, to the damage of the player. A little bye-play followed, and St George wound up the drama with:

Gentlemen and ladies! the sport is almost ended;
Come pay to the box, it is highly commended.
The box it would speak if it had but a tongue,
Come throw in your money, and think it no wrong.

This was 'very tragical mirth', but, as Theseus said, 'the worst are no worse if imagination amend them'.

Hamilton Jenkin, not to be left out, also described a mummers' play from about 1834: he gleaned his information from the antiquary William Sandys, who *wrote Specimens of Cornish Provincial Dialect* in 1846 under the pseudonym of 'Uncle Jan Trenoodle'.

It was a New Year's Eve, the writer tells us, and a goodly party of friends and neighbours was gathered to spend the day at 'Cousin Nic Carnoweth's'. After a dinner consisting of 'broth, a couple of nice pluffy young mabyers (pullets), a starry-gazy (pilchard) pie, a thumping figgy-pudding, and plenty of strong drink to keep out the cold', the company seated themselves round the Christmas stock blazing cheerfully on the open hearth. Towards 'teening time', or the fall of dusk, 'there came a grinning gaukum who told us as how the guise dancers were to the door, with the ancient play of St George. Gladly did we give them leave to enter, so in they came. There was old Feyther Chrestmas with a make-wise face possed (stuck) up on top of his own, and his long white wig, trapesing about and getting in his tantrums; and there was the Doctor, as they called 'un, with a three-cornered piked hat and his face all rudded and whited, with spurticles (spectacles) on top of his nause. And there was one in a maiden's bed-gownd and coat with ribbons, and a nackan (handkerchief) in his hand and a gook (sun bonnet) on his head. Other youngsters were in white, with ribbons tied all over their shirt sleeves, and with nackans and swords, and such caps as I never see'd before. They was half a fathom high, made of pastyboard (cardboard), weth powers (heaps) of beads and looking-glass, and shreds of old cloth strung upon slivers (strips) of pith – and they strutted about so brave as lubber cocks (turkey cocks)'.

And then they gave the word to begin, and old 'Feyther Chrestmas' stepped out and said:

> Here comes I, ould Feyther Chrestmas,
> Welcome or welcome not,
> I do hope ould Feyther Chrestmas
> Will never be forgot.

Father Christmas, having introduced the play, steps back into the half-circle of the performers, leaving the stage open for the Turkish knight. The latter struts forth in an arrogant fashion, proclaiming his superiority to any Christian knight, until, of a sudden, St George himself appears. He also is confident of his prowess, and in consequence a fight takes place in which the Turkish knight is knocked down for dead. Here the play seems like to have ended but for the timely intervention of the Doctor who, after a good deal of humorous 'gag', cures him of his 'deep and deadly wound'. Once more the Turkish knight arises to do battle, but he is speedily laid low by St George, and this time slain for good. Then in comes the Dragon, a fearsome-looking beast 'with long and scurvy jaw'. After a fitting display of his fearsome qualities, the Dragon also is slain by St George who, as a somewhat unexpected reward for his valour, is given the hand of 'Sabra, the King of Egypt's daughter', in marriage.

The Dragon is quite a rare character in British mummers' plays, although one appeared in a Surrey play as well as in the Cornish examples given above; he still struts his stuff in a 'revival' on the Kent/ Surrey border. In *Folklore of Cornwall* we described the plays as 'death and resurrection in doggerel' but added:

Cornish pantomime.

The Mullion play, which continued until the late nineteenth century, forswore the doggerel and was played in mime, true mumming; in Stithians, up to the outbreak of the First World War, their play's hero was not St George but simple Jack. Most of the lines were crude and ill-shaped but the Cadgwith play gave this verse to Father Christmas:

As I lay on my silent bed,
I dreamt my only son was dead.
Thou cruel monster, what hast thou done?
Thou'st ruined and killed my only son.

An extant photograph proves that Padstow maintained its play into the twentieth century; this play included a nautical character called Tom Bowling, who entered whilst playing an accordion and singing:

Here am I, Sailor Boy, just come from a-cruising;
I'll marry the girl and make her my wife
And go no more a-cruising.

Hamilton Jenkin charted the decline of mumming, recalling the comments of the clerical folklore collector W. Lach-Szyrma of Penzance:

> Although many years have elapsed since the 'St George' play ceased to be a regular feature of (the) midwinter carnival, it was not wholly forgotten. In 1866 the Rev W S Lach-Szyrma witnessed its performance by the miners of Pensilva, near Liskeard. In 1890 the villagers of Manaccan and St Martin-in-Meneage toured the play through their neighbourhood with great success. Another excellent rendering of the play was given by the boys of the Roskear School, at Camborne, during the Christmas of 1914. The intention, however, of making it an annual event was frustrated by the staff alterations caused by the war.

The First World War saw the demise of many traditional customs throughout Britain but, despite all the gloomy predictions, guising struggled on. In west Cornwall the BBC recorded the 'Turkey Rhubarb' dance in 1936, a recording now sadly lost; the accompanying rhyme, though, remains:

Turkey Rhubarb, Turkey Rhubarb, Turkey Rhubarb I sell,
I come here from Turkey to make you all well.

Don't you all know me? O my name it is Dan,
For I am the celebrated Turkey Rhubarb man.

The dance was a type of mazurka but it is tempting to connect 'Turkey Rhubarb' with the Turkish Knight of the mummers' plays. Turkey rhubarb, in fact, is a Chinese herb, *rheum palmatum*, not the common garden plant, and used as a cure for diarrhoea. Robert Morton Nance offers *tavol Turkey* for 'rhubarb' in the Cornish language.

Paul and Madron Women's Institute staged a mummers' play until the 1940s and, since then, revivals have been regular. We hope that Padstow's Mummers' Days will also continue to happen each year. To conclude, let the Trigg Morris Men of Bodmin have the final words from their mummers' play:

So now we make an ending,
Of what we did begin,
For going out a-guising
We think it is no sin.

FIGGY PUDDING

Here is a traditional Cornish alternative to Christmas pudding, from the Sally Shaw collection:

2oz self-raising flour;
2 figs, chopped well;
1 tbsp sherry
8oz raisins;
grated rind of 1 lemon;
a little milk.

4oz suet;
2 tsps allspice;
4oz breadcrumbs;
½oz sugar;
2 beaten eggs;

Mix all the dry ingredients together.

Stir in the eggs and sherry and add just enough milk to make a soft dough.

Place in a buttered pudding basin and cover with greaseproof paper, double thickness, allowing enough room for the pudding to swell.

Steam for 3½ hours and serve hot with a sherry sauce.

A CORNISH CHILDHOOD

By A.L. Rowse

Dr A.L. Rowse (1903-1997) was, perhaps, Cornwall's greatest literary figure of the twentieth century. Born in Tregonissey to a china-clay worker who boosted his income by running a shop, he rose above his humble origins by winning a scholarship to Christ Church College, Oxford. There he gained a first in modern history and became best known as an historian specialising in the Tudor period. He also wrote poetry, short stories and works of biography and autobiography, notably *A Cornish Childhood* (1942), possibly his finest achievement.

He stood unsuccessfully for Parliament as a Labour Party candidate before the Second World War but later turned sharply to the right. During his final years, he lived in Trenarren House, south of St Austell, which he had coveted since childhood: although close geographically to his family home, it was spiritually a million miles away.

> Even my father took part in the music which was the best part of their activities and which reached its high point with Christmas time, New Year and Twelfth Night. My father's instrument was a bass-viol – which mother did not like as it woke up the baby,

A.L. Rowse.

my sister Hilda; so he sold it and bought a harmonium, which was exchanged for a piano when she grew into girlhood – a nice example of change of taste and a degree of economic improvement. But he always had a concertina, too, right up into my boyhood, though by then he didn't play it much, and there was a banjo and a tambourine, I remember, among other instruments stowed away in the cupboard under the stairs. When I was a small child and he was not so deaf and morose as he became, he used to take me up on his knee, marking time with his foot, playing the banjo and singing:

Cornish children playing in the snow.

Nobody in the house but Dinah,
Nobody in the house I know;
Nobody in the house but Dinah,
Playing on the old banjo.

I used to find that curiously affecting; I wondered who the mysterious Dinah was: she was an occupant of my world, indeed a well-known figure in the landscape, though I had never seen her. I suppose in fact she was an American (Black) woman, and this song, about which I knew nothing, may have been picked up by his mining brothers in America or Africa – one or other of them was always going to and fro.

In fact, the song probably remained in Cornwall from one of the travelling minstrel shows that were popular there in the nineteenth century. It is still known to just about every Cornish male-voice choir, can be heard in pubs from Penzance to Bude and is part of Padstow's guising repertoire.

TRENARREN TOWARDS CHRISTMAS

By A.L. Rowse

As Menabilly was to Daphne Du Maurier, so was Trenarren to A.L. Rowse: it was the house of his dreams, set in solitary splendour in the south Cornish countryside. Rowse was not a great poet but he is at his best in this idyll.

How to describe the stillness, the planetary
Perfection of this moment caught and held;
The face of the moon meshed in the branches
Beholds me; quartz sparkles in the ground,
Latticed shadows on white gravel,
The skeleton of the insignis pine;
Billowing clouds move eastward
Out over the bay under a resplendent
Three-quarters moon and one attendant
Star. In the west the screen of trees
Filters the night, and the world moves on
Towards Christmas, as my night moves on
To its term. The thought of those here before me
Inhabits the moonlit scene – the taciturn

Colonel, pacing the terrace with his gun,
The former peacocks with their raucous cry,
And all those visitants who now have gone,
The farmer's boy, handsome as Antinous,
Moody and sullen, drowned in his bravery
Upon the beach. Ghostly *revenants* mostly
Appear on the terrace in the white moonlight,
Present themselves to the mind to punctuate
The vanished irrecoverable years;
The shelving lawn, the signal pine,
The bay all silver in the moon, in beauty
More rare than ever in its solitude,
All that is wanting is love fulfilled.

OF GHOULIES AND GHOSTIES

Cornwall is a land of ghosts. Bottrell describes the savage end of the Penrose family from Sennen, where murder and mayhem was disclosed by the arrival of a spectral ship on Christmas Eve. Writing in 1880, he also recalls this cautionary tale from Pendeen; *vow*, incidentally, is a corruption of the Cornish *fogou*, meaning 'cave':

> At dawn on Christmas-day the spirit of the 'Vow' has frequently been seen just within the entrance (of the) cave, in the form of a beautiful lady dressed in white, with a red rose in her mouth. There were persons living a few years since who had seen the fair but not less fearful vision; for disaster was sure to visit those who intruded on the spirit's morning airing.

Mrs Bonham, in *Christmas in Cornwall* 60 *Years Ago*, tells a more credible 'ghost' story. It is interesting to speculate whether she chose the name 'Billy Bottrell' in ironic deference to William Bottrell himself.

> Every village in Cornwall had its own particular ghosts, and St Cadge was no exception to the rule, its ghost appearing, as was meet and right, one Christmas Eve. But we must go back a few years in order to make things plain.

Billy Bottrell and Betty Coade were a quiet-going pair during their courtship. Betty, who lived in farm service, always said that once a week, namely, Sunday, was often enough for any decent young woman to see her 'shiner'; and no mistress, we may be sure, would dispute that matter with her. Folks said that Billy was not very bright, and that Betty, fairly good-looking and a capital servant, might do better; but she was pleased with her choice, and that settled it.

Christmas Eve, the day before the wedding, had arrived, and Billy in great glee clapped his hands, grinned, and leaped about like one demented. 'Ah!' he exclaimed exultingly to some friends, 'I'm Billy Bottrell to-day, I shall be William Coade to-morrow.' His brain was in a whirl, and he had somehow mixed things up.

Billy and Betty began housekeeping in a long, low, thatched building containing only one large room. There was a lovely view of St Cadge cove and cliffs from the cottage, though doubtless the inmates thought little of that.

The surplus vegetables from their large garden partly provided a pig, which they would feed up for killing. Billy's idea of feeding a pig was a novel one, for it had a feast one day, and a fast the next, so as to make streaky pork, as he used to say.

Time went on till the cottage swarmed with children. Betty had decent ideas, and she worried over so many sleeping in one room that served for every purpose. She soon conceived a plan, bought a few laths and some thin lengths of wood, and then with her own hands fixed up two or three partitions to form cubicles. These partitions she covered with newspapers, begged from the respectable farmers for miles around, for in those days papers were scarce, costing fourpence halfpenny and even sixpence each.

After great exertions she managed to secure a little privacy for the elder children, though her achievement only consisted of a very frail structure; so that one morning, when there was a strong southerly wind blowing directly against Betty's door, and Mr Collins, wishing to speak to Billy, lifted the latch and opened it, a blast swept through the interior, and the papered partitions rattled and quivered like aspen-leaves.

'Aw! my dear saul!' cried Betty in great alarm; 'shut the doer, quick – shut'n, ar my screens will be down all of a heap.'

Billy's wages were small, but the large family managed somehow to get along on them, supplemented occasionally by a little smuggling job.

In course of time the elder boys went into farm service and times grew somewhat better.

One Christmas Eve just seventeen years after Billy's wedding, Jackman the eldest boy came home very ill; and Billy thinking him in danger rode off on a borrowed horse for the doctor, who prescribed, gave Betty her orders and left.

Mother and father had passed an exciting day, and as the boy now quietly slept, they left him in charge of his elder sister, and hurried down to the 'White Goose' to have a little drop before the house was closed.

Young Collins, and his friend Joe Bennett, always ready for any fun, listened while the story of Jackman's sudden illness was related for the good of every one in the kitchen, and then the two young men slipped out. Their plans were soon formed, and both creeping under an old hedge, that near the ground had been dug out, they waited in a crouching position, their backs to the road, and each with a white garment drawn over the extremity nearest to any passer-by. In a few minutes they heard footsteps coming up the hill.

'Wha's that, Betty, up theere in the 'edge?' asked Billy, tremblingly.

'Wheere, Billy?'

'Why, up theere – look.'

'Law, whatever es et? Why 'tes aw tooken, Billy, Jackman'll die, I knaw aw will. They're ghoostes.'

'No, no, Betty,' he replied reassuringly, though himself trembling with fear. 'they're two white pigs,' and he approached cautiously, feeling before him with his stick, but still keeping at some distance. 'Aw hooay – aw hooay,' he cried out to the pigs.

The two young men, after allowing him to call and beat his stick on the ground for a minute or two, without in the least altering the position of their bodies, hopped out of the hedge, and to the horror of the frightened couple hopped away down the hill. And such ghostly sights they looked in the partial darkness that Betty in great distress cried out: 'Aw, Billy, my dear boy'll die. Iss aw will, thus aw tooken chul tha's what that es.'

They were riveted to the spot with fear. Meanwhile the merry youths were no sooner out of sight, than, scampering through the village, they climbed some hedges, ran up the fields, and planted themselves, white backs outwards, near a path along which the couple had to pass to get to their cottage.

At last, partially recovered from their terrible fright, Billy and Betty came slowly up the hill, talking quietly and solemnly. They got over the stile, and there, before them, was the strange vision once more!

'Oh! my goodness guide me, Billy, what shall es do? theere's the ghoostes agen. Oh! wheere shall I go? Lem me shut my eyes. Oh! Billy, catch hawld of me – Oh! Now we do knaw 'tes two ghoostes, 'cause they was down bottom of the hill jest now, an' now they're up 'long here.'

The ghosts once more went hop, hop, down the field, where the horrified couple rushed wildly one after the other, Betty screaming at the top of her voice, and on reaching the cottage, forgetting

Jackman, she beat wildly on the door, arousing the poor boy from his peaceful sleep; and then she sank down on the floor and almost fainted away.

The tale of the two ghosts seen on Christmas Eve went the round of St Cadge and its neighbourhood, and was told, not always without exaggeration of its horrors, to many a shuddering circle round the Christmas fire when the carol-singing was over: but the ghosts themselves laughed in their sleeves and kept their secret for years.

SOME OLD CORNISH FOLK

By Salome Hocking

Salome Hocking (1859-1927) was the younger sister of the prolific writing brothers Silas and Joseph Hocking. They were born in St Stephen-in-Brannel, near St Austell, but Salome, after marrying the publisher Arthur Fifield in 1894, lived in Surrey until she died. Whilst there she added to her five early novels with at least four more works, including *Some Old Cornish Folk* (1903), recollections of her previous neighbours in St Stephen. This tale, like Mrs Bonham's ghost story, reflects the casual cruelty of the time:

> There is no one who loves a humorous, well-told story better than a Cornishman. It does not matter even if the story tells against him; if it is kindly done, he will enjoy it. But once let him think (if you are a stranger) that you ar laughing at him, and he will withdraw himself inside his shell as completely as a snail when its horns are touched. With his own countrymen, however, he will hit back without mercy. This reminds me of a story I heard only a short time ago of two men who were both rather afflicted. One had had his nose broken by the kick of a horse, and the other had lost an ear. They both spoke broad Cornish. It was New Year's Eve; and

as they passed each other on the road, the one with the defective nose sang out cheerily:

'Appy new 'ear to ee, matey.'

'Appy new noase to you,' was the snappish reply.

FAITHFUL JANE

By Sir Arthur Quiller Couch

In his 1988 biography, A.L. Rowse described Sir Arthur Quiller Couch (1863-1944) – 'Q' to his many admirers – as 'half-Cornish, half-English'. Certainly, his mother was Devonian but his heart was always true to Cornwall. Q was born in Bodmin but it was nearby Fowey which became the 'Troy Town' of his fiction and where most of his best work was set. He created the Cambridge School of English Literature and, as one of the greatest anthologists of his time, edited the first *Oxford Book of English Verse*. He wrote literary criticism, much of it still relevant, a collection of mostly forgettable novels, poetry and a vast number of some of the best short stories in the English language. Today, Q is largely neglected: it is surely time for a renaissance of interest.

The extract here concludes a rather sad tale of an engagement prolonged by class tension. It first appeared in the *Times* of 24 December 1937, and is remarkable for featuring a sympathetic lawyer. 'Reselda' is recognisable as Polruan, across the estuary from Fowey.

A post-mortem revealed that John Berrycombe had died of fatty degeneration of the heart.

He was buried as he had wished, in Reselda churchyard. Custom in Reselda parish forbade women, if related or nearly concerned, to attend funerals. So Jane and Emma, having pulled down the house blinds, sought the parlour at first note from the tolling-bell, and sat the time out in silence.

Towards next afternoon (Christmas Eve) a hired vehicle descended the steep hill to 'The Norseman's Arms'. At a bend of the road below Reselda church it had passed the village schoolhouse ablaze with lights and ringing with the indoor noise and merriment of children.

At the 'Norseman's' porch it disgorged three passengers, whom Emma Peascod ushered into the parlour, where Mr Attley sat with John's will open before him under the lamp. He rose and, bowing, indicated chairs. Mrs Burslade (nee Matilda Berrycombe), a stoutish matron in flounces of black crepe, sank upon the small sofa and lifted her veil upon a face in which the very sharp eyes pierced a plaster of enamel. Miles Berrycombe seated himself, with back stiff as a ramrod, on Mr Attley's right. The Reverend Coningsby Berrycombe, after a glance around, settled himself beside his sister.

'I should apologize for Miss Trewman,' said the solicitor. 'She has just returned from a children's Christmas-tree, and will be here in a minute or two. Here is a copy, Mr Miles, of the will, as promised when you called on me this morning.'

Miles Berrycombe took the copy, spread it, and adjusted his glasses.

'A Christmas-tree, did you say?' shrilled Mrs Burslade from the sofa. 'And dear John scarcely cold in his grave! Well, of all - .'

But at that moment Jane entered, dressed quietly in grey. With an inclination of her head she comprehended the visitors, and, moving to the fire-place, stood facing them.

'These gentlemen, Miss Trewman, and their sister desire a talk with you respecting their brother's will. The relevant sentence, Mr Miles, is plain enough and concise?'

'Quite!'

'After a few legacies the testator leaves – here are the words – 'the residue of my worldly estate to my dear wife, Jane Berrycombe, absolutely and at her sole use and disposition.' Those were his own words: he insisted on them.'

'Yes, of course, of course – no reflection at all upon you, Mr Attley. Every man his own lawyer, eh? But' – pricking the paper with his pencil – 'here is the point, Miss Trewman. Were you my brother's wife at the date of his signing?'

'Of course not.'

Mr Attley interposed. 'The Court, sir – if that be your ground, and I have suspected it since this morning – would almost certainly take account of plainly declared intentions. And seeing that the parties' banns were out as recently as last Sunday, I shall positively advise my client - .'

Jane broke in. 'Your pardon, dear Mr Attley; but I shan't take anyone's advice in this. I knew John's intentions well enough, though in these years never told. These people want to dispute the will: but they have something at back of their minds, and 'twill save time if they speak it out.'

'To come to the point, then,' said Miles Berrycombe after a pause, choosing his words, 'we are certainly inclined to question the validity –'

'Tut!' interposed Mr Attley.

' – but we have consulted. The estate will probably realise seventy thousand pounds (I put this not too optimistically, Mr Attley). And, if in consideration of your natural disappointment, one thousand down or perhaps an annuity - .'

Jane had turned to a small mirror above the chimneypiece, and seemed to be studying the lines of her face in it while she spoke to it, slowly:

'Mr Attley, you are a gentleman, and would work for my rights on your honour's sake. But there's two sorts of pride – one that has ruined the best of John's life and mine, and another that stamps on it and all such: and that sort happens to be mine. The best service in life you can ever do me is here and now; to show these people to the door.' She put a hand in her bodice and pulled out a wad of notes. 'Tell them I'll never touch a penny of Berrycombe money and let them take this.' She put out her hand behind her. 'John gave it to me to spend in setting up house. I haven't spent a penny of it.'

'Well, and that's over!' said Jane to Emma half an hour later. 'Let's fit and have a cup of tea.'

'Highly satisfactory I call it, and a credit in a way to all concerned,' said the Reverend Coningsby Berrycombe after dinner that evening, as he held up a glass of John's forty-five port against the candlelight.

'Though,' said his sister, 'I can never forget the impudent way that woman carried it off.....Hark!'

Outside the lit windows, in the drive, a chorus of childish voices had started to trill:

'Good Christian friends rejoice,

With heart and soul and voice ... '

SOUND, SOUND

Christmas carols specific to a local area were not, until recent years, particularly rare; some still remain in parts of Yorkshire. In Cornwall, Redruth, St Ives, Morwenstow and St Keverne, amongst others, have their own sets, now largely forgotten. Padstow, though, that hotbed of tradition, retains its carols. Every Saturday in December, Padstow's streets and harbour resound with the old songs, at the instruction 'Strike sound!' Mostly, the carols date from the nineteenth century: some are locally made, both words and music; others written by well-known hymnsters like Thomas Merritt. All – certainly in these versions – are unknown outside Padstow, where the superb harmony singing has to be heard to be truly appreciated. The songs were set down and published in 1971 by John Worden, in a volume entitled *Strike Sound*, from which this carol is taken.

Sound, sound your instruments of joy:
To triumph shake each string,
To triumph shake each string.
Let shouts of universal joy
Welcome the new-born king,
Welcome the new-born king,

Welcome the new-born king,
Welcome the new-born king.

See, see the gladdening dawn appears:
Bright angels deck the morn,
Bright angels deck the morn.
Behold the great I AM is given:
The King of Glory's born,
The King of Glory's born, etc.

Surprising scene, stupendous love:
The Lord of Life descends,
The Lord of Life descends;
He left his glorious realms above
To be the sinners' friend,
To be the sinners' friend, etc.

Let heaven and earth and sea proclaim
His wondrous love abroad,
His wondrous love abroad
And all the universal frame
Sing praises to our God,
Sing praises to our God, etc.

Sound, sound your in - stru - ments of joy: To tri - umph shake each string
To tri - umph shake each string. Let shouts of u - ni - ver - sal joy
Welcome the new-born
Wel-come the new-born king, Wel - come the new - born king.
king, Welcome the new-born king, Wel - come the new - born king.

RICHARD TREVITHICK'S CHRISTMAS

Richard Trevithick was born in Illogan, near Camborne, in 1771 and died, nearly penniless, in Dartford, Kent, sixty-two years later. In between, he became Cornwall's – perhaps the world's – most famous engineer, inventor of the steam locomotive and saviour of mining in South America. The passage below is quoted in Anthony Burton's excellent *Richard Trevithick: Giant of Steam*, published in 2000, but appeared originally in *Life* magazine, as a quotation from 'old Stephen Williams' of Hayle:

> In the year 1801, upon Christmas-eve, coming on evening, Captain Dick got up steam, out in the high-road, just outside the shop at the Weith. When we get see'd that Captain Dick was agoing to turn on steam, we jumped up as many as could; may be seven or eight of us. 'Twas a stiffish hill going from the Weith up to Camborne Beacon, but she went off like a little bird.
>
> When she had gone about a quarter of a mile, there was a roughish piece of road covered with loose stones; she didn't go quite so fast, and as it was a flood of rain, and we were very squeezed together, I jumped off. She was going faster than I could

Goin' up Camborne 'ill.

walk, and went on up the hill about a quarter or a half a mile farther, when they turned her and came back again to the shop.

And so Christmas ushered in the age of steam.

OF MISERY AND MARRIAGE

It is, perhaps, time to recall that the Christmas period is not always one of sweetness and light. This harrowing report from the *West Briton* for Christmas Day, 1812, proves the point, dismissing at a stroke the myth of 'the good old days':

> There is now living near the village of Chacewater, a poor but once industrious man, named Hannibal Thomas, who has for two years past, laboured under that most dreadful of maladies, mental derangement. This unfortunate man, with his wife and five small children, has been chiefly supported by the parish for some time. On Thursday se'nnight, by the death of one of the children, the deplorable state of this miserable family was discovered. In the single room which they inhabit, the father was found confined to the bed, raving in all the wildness of frenzy; the mother also was confined by illness, and near her lay the corpse of her infant; and the other children crying for food, which their wretched parent was unable to supply, their pittance not enabling them to secure a sufficiency of barley-bread or potatoes. At this season of almost general festivity, their case is recommended to the attention of those whose hearts feel for human misery.

One hopes that the above scenario never befell the participants in the following saga, whose relationship began just one year after the Chacewater tragedy. This report, too, is taken from the *West Briton*, of Christmas Day, 1835:

> Married on Wednesday week, at St Gluvias, Mr John Taylor, hind (estate manager) at Scorrier, to Miss Ann Tredwen, of Penryn, after a courtship of 22 years, during which time the bridegroom married two others.

Margaret Courtney's description of a Christmas fair may echo Thomas Hardy's *The Mayor of Casterbridge*:

> In the week after Christmas-day a fair is held at Launceston ... called 'giglet fair' (a 'giglet or giglot' is a giddy young woman). It is principally attended by young people.

Wife selling was not unknown at Cornish fairs, certainly until the mid-1850s: thus Miss Courtney's next remarks, quoted from an early guide-book, could be less innocent than they appear:

> At this 'giglet market', or wife-market, the rustic swain was privileged with self-introduction to any of the nymphs around him, so that he had a good opportunity of choosing a suitable partner if tired of a single life.

A CORNISH YEAR

By C.C. Vyvyan

Here is another charming and optimistic piece by Lady Vyvyan, this time from a reflective book written in 1958:

> For the young it is natural to be optimistic when Christmas, with its gifts, festivities and merriment, is shining ahead like the Promised Land. Even on ourselves, the old ones, Christmas does exercise a steady magnetism. 'Three weeks today,' we murmur to ourselves, or 'Only a fortnight left, I shall never get through it all.' We even find it in our hearts to admire those tiresome models of foresight and carefulness, the insufficiently occupied ones, who begin in April to knit scarves for Christmas presents, buy their cards in September and boast of having every gift packed up before November is out.
>
> As for ourselves, we are plunged at the eleventh hour into a world of string, brown paper parcels and gaily coloured cards; also into a world of memories, for we know that what we call in Cornwall 'The Christmas' will carry us back in thought through all the years to our earliest impressions and experiences.
>
> There are childhood memories; waking very early in the dark in a state of tense excitement, with the single thought 'Christmas has come at last' and crawling over one's blankets to the foot of the bed

and groping round the leg of the stocking and feeling in the toe something that must surely be a fat orange and then lying awake guessing about all the other treasures stuffed inside. A whole day of toys and sweets and brightly coloured objects with never, from the grown-ups, any 'Don'ts' and never a 'You're-not-old-enough-for-that' and never a reference to 'Little Pitchers' while they were talking secrets. A whole day with no sharp answers like 'Wait and see' or 'Do as you're told' and not even any warnings like 'You'll eat yourself sick.' The children's own day. A day of surprises, with fruits and sweets everywhere and second helpings of all the best things. Then the tree with glittering ornaments and candles and Father Christmas with a sack full of presents and so, in the end, to bed with the strange feeling of being tired out with happiness.

Then there are later memories of Christmas after careers and marriages have split families asunder and have separated friends, when each anniversary bring reunions with sharper remembrance of the absent ones. It would be a day for allowing full play to feelings habitually repressed, to gestures of kindness towards all one's fellow-men. It would also be a day of warmth in remembering and being remembered by all who were loved best, not with a mere passing thought or two but with slow, lingering pleasure, like the pleasure of sipping an old wine quietly. The cards and greetings, the toasts drunk, the gifts exchanged would be merely symbols of these feelings but the symbols would all help to strengthen a belief that it really is love that makes the world go round.

So we come to the old age Christmas and when the toast is called for absent friends we falter now for a moment, remembering that so many of our absent ones can never more return. Then we give ourselves up again to the business of rejoicing with the young and recalling all the love that we have known throughout the years.

Yes, there is no doubt that Christmas Day is the most important anniversary in the whole year; it is a day that has its influence on heathen and on Christian peoples, transforming the Scrooges of this world, temporarily, into kind and generous men; promoting peace and goodwill, for this one day, in our troubled universe; increasing the friendliness of friends and burying the grudges of enemies; affording to children merriment that is unlimited and uncontrolled.

FUN AND GAMES

Margaret Courtney described many of the games played in Cornwall at Christmastide. She quoted from the *Cornishman* newspaper for 1881, with graphic details of a form of rounders played on the beach at St Ives which would probably enhance a modern Summer Olympics. Then she surpassed the Olympics Movement with some practices that would leave solo synchronised swimming for dead:

> Twelfth-day (old Christmas-day) was a time of general feasting and merriment. Into the Twelfth-day cake were put a wedding-ring, a sixpence (2½p), and a thimble. It was cut into as many portions as there were guests; the person who found the wedding-ring in his (or her) portion would be married before the year was out; the holder of the thimble would never be married, and the one who got the sixpence would die rich. After candlelight many games were played around the open fires. I will describe one:- 'Robin's alight'. A piece of stick was set on fire, and whirled rapidly in the hands of the first player, who repeated the words –
>
> 'Robin's alight, and if he go out I'll saddle your back.'
>
> It was then passed on, and the person who let the spark die had to pay a forfeit. – (West Cornwall.)
>
> The game in East Cornwall was known as 'Jack's alive'.

'Jack's alive and likely to live,
If he die in my hand a pawn I'll give.'

In this county forfeits are always called 'pawns'; they are cried by the holder of them, saying –

'Here's a pawn and a very pretty pawn!
And what shall the owner of this pawn do?'

After the midnight supper, at which in one village in the extreme West a pie of four-and-twenty blackbirds always appeared, many spells to forecast the future were practised. The following account of them was given to me by a friend. He says – 'I engaged in them once at Sennen ... with a lot of girls, but as my object was only to spoil sport and make the girls laugh or speak, it was not quite satisfactory. I suppose the time to which I refer is over forty years ago (pre 1850). After making up a large turf fire, for hot 'umers' (embers) and pure water are absolutely necessary in these divinations, the young people silently left the house in single file, to pull the rushes and gather the ivy-leaves by means of which they were to learn whether they were to be married, and to whom; and if any, or how many, of their friends were to die before the end of the year. On leaving and on returning each of these Twelfth-night diviners touched the 'cravel' with the forehead and 'wished'. The cravel is the tree that preceded lintels in chimney corners, and its name from this custom may have been derived from the verb 'to crave'. Had either of the party inadvertently broken the silence before the rushes and ivy-leaves had been procured they would all have been obliged to retrace their steps to the house and again touch the cravel; but this time all went well. When we came back those who wished to know their fate named the rushes in pairs, and placed them in the hot embers: one or two of the engaged couples being too shy to do this for themselves, their friends, amidst much laughing, did it for them. The manner in which the rushes burned showed if the young couple were to be married to the person chosen or not: some, of course, burnt well, others parted, and one or two went out altogether. The couples that burnt smoothly were to be wedded, and the one named after the rush that lasted longest outlived the other. This settled, one ivy-leaf was thrown on the fire; the number of cracks it made was the number of years before the wedding would take place. Then two were placed on the hot ashes; the cracks they gave this time showed how many children the two would have. We then drew ivy-leaves named after present or absent friends through a wedding-ring, and put them into a basin of water which we left until the next morning. Those persons whose leaves had shrivelled or turned black in the night were to die before the next Twelfth-tide, and those who were so unfortunate as to find their leaves spotted with red, by some violent death, unless a 'pellar' (wise man) could by his skill and incantations grant protection. These prophecies through superstition sometimes unluckily fulfilled themselves.'

During the twelve days of Christmas card-playing was a very favourite amusement with all classes. Whilst the old people enjoyed their game of whist with 'swabbers', the young ones had their round games. I will append the rules of two or three for those who would like to try them.

Whist (or whisk, as I have heard an old lady call it and maintain that that was its proper name) with 'swabbers'.

This game, which was played as recently as 1880, nightly, by four maiden ladies at Falmouth, is like ordinary whist; but each player before beginning to play puts into the pool a fixed sum for 'swabs'. The 'swab-cards' are – ace and deuce of trumps, ace of hearts and knave of clubs. The four cards are of equal value; but should hearts be trumps the ace would count double.

'Board-'em', a round game that can be played by any number of players, from two to eight; it is played for fish, and there must never be less than six fish in the pool. Six cards are dealt to each person;

and the thirteenth, if two are playing, the nineteenth if three, and so on, is turned up for trumps. The fore-hand plays; the next player, if he has one, must follow suit, if not, he may play another suit, or trump. The highest card of the original suit, if not trumped, takes the trick and one or more fish, according to the number staked. If you have neither card in your hand that you think will make a trick you may decline to play, in which case you only lose your stake; but should you play and fail to take a trick you pay for the whole company, and are said to 'be boarded'.

'Ranter-go-round' was formerly played in four divisions marked with chalk upon a tea-tray; or even, in some cases, on a bellows – it is now played upon a table, and is called 'Miss Joan'. Any number of players may join in it. The first player throws down any card of any suit, and says:-

'Here's a .....as you may see.

2nd Player – Here's another as good as he.

3rd Player – And here's the best of all the three.

4th Player – And here's Miss Joan, come to tickle me.'

The holder of the fourth card wins the trick. He sometimes added the words wee-wee; but these are now generally omitted. If the person sitting next to the fore-hand has neither one of the cards demanded (one of the same value as the first played, in another suit), he pays one to the pool, as must all in turn who fail to produce the right cards. The player of the third may have the fourth in his hand, in which case all the others pay. The holder of the most tricks wins the game and takes the pool.

I once, about thirty years since, at this season of the year, joined some children at Camborne who were playing a very primitive game called by them 'pinny-ninny'. A basin turned upside-down was placed in the centre of a not very large round table. The players were supplied with small piles of pins – not the well-made ones

A game of cards. (From an old engraving)

> sold in papers, but clumsy things with wire heads – 'round-pins'. A large bottle full of them might, then, always be seen in the general shop window of every little country village. Each in turn dropped a pin over the side of the basin, and he whose pin fell and formed a cross on the top of the heap was entitled to add them to his own pile. This went on until one player had beggared all the others. Poor children before Christmas often begged pins to play this game, and their request was always granted by the gift of two.

Today, these games have been replaced by flashy equivalents from the major manufacturers but it is doubtful that children gain greater enjoyment from them. Even 'the general shop window of every little country village' is a thing of the past.

In our *Folklore of Cornwall* (2003) we described an ancient custom that degenerated into a Christmas sport:

> The ceremony of Hunting the Wren still survives in Ireland and the Isle of Man, albeit in an emasculated form, with an effigy replacing the live bird; in Cornwall it continued into the last century as a general 'bird-shoot', on St Stephen's (Boxing) Day, when it was unwise to be out in the lanes, with indiscriminate gunfire all around. The original ceremony may be explained as a punishment for the wren, which awakened St Stephen's prison guards as the saint was about to make his escape from captivity. A second explanation is that, when St Paul was converted, the evil side of his character took refuge in a wren's body. Since then the birds have become so vicious that, unless killed, they would destroy every creature smaller than themselves.

Only traffic endangers the unwary Christmas rambler in today's Cornish lanes.

JOHN PENROSE

By J.C. Tregarthen

Born in Penzance in 1855, John Coulson Tregarthen was of a Scillonian family: indeed, Tregarthens remains a popular hotel on St Mary's. He was elected a Bard of the Cornish Gorsedd and attended the first ever Gorsedd, held at Boscawen-Un in 1928; he took as his Bardic name Mylgarer, 'Lover of Wild Animals', and most of his books concentrated on animal life. While his tales of badgers, otters, hares and foxes smack of anthropomorphism, he was never afraid of showing life 'red in tooth and claw'; his splendid *Wild Life at the Land's End* remains unequalled in its genre. The novel *John Penrose* (1923) reflects Tregarthen's interest in wildlife, plus a deep knowledge of Cornish culture. While not, perhaps, a great work of literature, it is racy and continues to hold the reader's interest: no mean epitaph for a regional writer who died in 1933.

'Then you will come to us the day after Christmas Day?'

'We shall be delighted, shall we not, granfer?'

'Iss, my dear, I'm always ready to go to Jack's.'

'And now, Loveday,' I said, 'I want to ask another favour. May I bring the handbell ringers here tomorrow after leaving the mansion?'

'Do, I should love to be serenaded like the princess in a fairy story; I will be sure to be awake if you come before midnight.'

'We will be here before then.'

And as the mansion clock was striking eleven, we ringers, to the number of sixteen, passed the Carn on the way to Forest Carn, where we formed up round Oliver Gendall, who held the lantern and beat the time as we rang, 'I saw Three Ships come sailing by', 'The Farmer's Boy', 'Good King Wenceslas', 'Noel', 'God rest you, Merry Gentlemen'.

Then, as at the mansion, we sang, 'Hark, the herald angels sing'.

In the silence that followed, Loveday came to the window, and said, 'One and all, I thank you.'

To discover the fate of Jack and Loveday, you should read the novel, which was re-published in 2004.

THE SAINT DAY CAROL

This beautiful version of *The Holly and the Ivy* was collected in the early twentieth century from Thomas Beard, aged between fifty and sixty, of St Day, near Redruth. His ancestors had sung the carol for generations before him and so it was named after his home village. The final verse was added later. Douglas Brice, in *The Folk Carol of England* (1967), wrote that the original song 'is a truly remarkable carol, for in the short space of six lines it covers the theology of the Immaculate Conception, the Incarnation and the Act of Redemption'. Adding that the holly signifies 'man' while the ivy is 'woman', Brice concludes that 'the meaning of the carol is clear: 'Christ in His innocence was the Second Adam come to restore to Mankind the innocence it had lost'.

Now the holly bears a berry as white as the milk
And Mary bore Jesus all wrapped up in silk;
And Mary bore Jesus our Saviour for to be
And the first tree in the greenwood it was the holly:
Holly, holly,
And the first tree in the greenwood it was the holly.

Now the holly bears a berry as green as the grass
And Mary bore Jesus who died on the cross;
Refrain.

Now the holly bears a berry as black as the coal
And Mary bore Jesus who died for us all;
Refrain.

Now the holly bears a berry as blood it was red
And Mary bore Jesus who rose from the dead;
Refrain.

EARLY TIDE: A MEVAGISSEY CHILDHOOD

By Mary Lakeman

Mary Harriet Lakeman was a Mevagissey fisherman's daughter, born in the village in 1911. A schoolteacher by profession, she wrote her sharp evocation of early twentieth- century life in 1978, and died in 1981. She is notable for not sharing her fellow Cornishmen's uncritical love of Christmas carols:

> There remains Christmas, and I do not remember any community celebrations as such except for carols in chapel; those carols which recurred so mechanically. To my sorrow I have never received sympathy from anyone in my dislike of the rumbustious character of some of them. Only at the plaintive strains of 'In the bleak midwinter Frosty wind made moan' was my heart touched, and I find this little gem to have been the joint effort of Gustav Holst and Christina Rossetti.
>
> I got a deal of pleasure sitting with my elbows on the kitchen table watching Mother and Dollie make puddings and cakes. Those were the only cookery lessons I have ever had, my *Cordon Bleu* complete, absorbed unconsciously while talking of other things and eating the odd raisin or bit of peel.

Boats at Mevagissey.

When Marj and I were in the Christmas stocking stage, our six brothers and sisters had passed well beyond it, and in consequence we were early disillusioned about the real identity of Father Christmas. Already uneasily aware of the truth, Marj remembers hearing Mother groan on the landing outside our bedroom door. On her way to bed, wearied with Christmas preparations she cried, 'Oh my dear life I haven't filled the cheeld's stocking.'

'This,' though Marj to herself, 'is the end. I must tell Mother not to be bothered with it next year.'

Sometimes the boys went wild using the half filled stockings to give us a friendly clout, and we all suddenly joined in a game of derision of stockings so scantily packed and with only an orange and an apple to give them weight. In a sense we have played that game ever since, inimical as we are to pretence of any kind, and without expectation or indeed a desire for presents.

Once Marj's stocking got lost, but it turned up later in a cupboard, and we gleefully shared the contents savouring the taste of Christmas fruit in mid-January.

CHRISTMAS CRACKERS: A MISCELLANY

The old Cornish Christmas involved a rich medley of folklore and fun. In this section we will weave together a selection of choice titbits. For instance, although Cornwall is not widely known for Morris dancing (*pace* Trigg Morris of Bodmin), one of the earliest references to Christmas Morris dancing appears in the domestic accounts for Lanherne, in St Mawgan-in-Pydar, for the winter of 1466-67. Among the listed items are eight quires of paper and five ells of Holland cloth for disguise, plus four dozen bells. The dance was obviously an important part of Lanherne's and, by inference, the gentry's Christmas and it is perhaps time for England to take its national dance seriously.

As proof of the temperate nature of the Cornish climate at Christmas, the *West Briton* printed the following report on New Year's Day, 1861:

> In order to practically illustrate the calmness of the weather at the Land's End on Christmas eve and Christmas day, a person lighted a candle, in the open air, at Trevescan, on Christmas eve, and carried it to the church, a distance of about half-a-mile, where four others were lighted and placed on each of the pinnacles of the church-tower. This was done about eleven o'clock at night, and the candles

> continued burning until two o'clock on the following morning, when the same candle that was carried to the church was again re-lighted, and carried back to Trevescan. No person living in the locality can ever remember such a thing being done before, thus affording a practical and novel instance of the serenity of the atmosphere around the usually-boisterous 'dark Bolerium, seat of storms', of the poet.

Margaret Courtney, writing in 1890, pointed out that the practice was not new:

> In a few remote districts on Christmas-eve children may be, after nightfall, occasionally (but rarely) found dancing around painted lighted candles placed in a box of sand. This custom was very general fifty years ago. The church towers, too, are sometimes illuminated. This, of course, on the coast can only be done in very calm weather. The tower of Zennor church ... was lit up in 1883, for the first time since 1866.

She also recalled the forerunners of decorations and of kissing under the mistletoe:

> In Cornwall ... houses are at Christmas 'dressed up' with evergreens, sold in small bunches, called 'Penn'orths of Chris'mas'; and two hoops fastened one in the other by nails at the centres are gaily decorated with evergreens, apples, oranges, &c., and suspended from the middle beam in the ceiling of the best kitchen. This is the 'bush', or 'kissing bush'. At night a lighted candle is put in it, stuck on the bottom nail; but once or twice lately I have seen a Chinese lantern hanging from the top one.

Holly was known as 'the Cornish Christmas tree' and was never burned, to avoid bad luck: miners wore it on their helmets and fishermen hung it from their masts as Christmas approached. Hamilton Jenkin was expansive on the subject. This was written in 1934, only one year after Hitler came to power in Germany, when there was, perhaps, an anti-German feeling rising in Britain: hence, his Christmas tree jibe.

> ... were (the modern Cornishman's) ancestors to return once more to their beloved land they would still find even in the dying embers of a modern Cornish Christmas other features besides the carols to remind them of the past. Amongst these should be mentioned the picturesque custom of hanging up the Christmas 'bush'. The latter, when properly constructed, consists of two little wooden hoops fastened one into the other at right angles, the framework thus formed being decorated with evergreens, furze blossom, apples, oranges, etc. This pleasing form of decoration, which is known in some districts as the 'kissing bush', is usually suspended in the front window of the house, and when illuminated at night by a lighted candle set inside it, has a peculiarly festive appearance. Considering how easily and cheaply the bush can be made, it is regrettable that this old British form of decoration should have been so widely supplanted by its German counterpart – the Christmas tree.
>
> In the days when open hearths were still universal in the farmhouses, the burning of the Christmas 'stock' (as the 'Yule-log' of other parts of Britain was known in Cornwall) was not without its ceremonial. In many cases the stocks had the figure of a man roughly chalked upon them, and were often ignited with a piece of charred wood which had been saved from the last year's fire. A curious story relating to one of these logs is told in an early number of the *West Briton* newspaper. One evening during the Christmas of

A Cornish cottage at Christmas.

> 1838 a certain Mr Lukey, of Carminow, near Helston, was sitting by the fire when his ears were suddenly assailed by cries resembling those of a child which apparently proceeded from the chimney wherein the stock lay burning – 'as it had been for three successive days, according to the universal custom of the country folk at this season'. On examining the log he noticed that it contained a little hole, which being too small to admit his fingers he split open with an axe, only to discover to his great astonishment a large toad entombed in the centre!

The Yule Log in Cornwall was more commonly known as a 'mock'. Traditionally, the spriggans were a race of grotesquely-ugly warrior fairies but, here, Robert Hunt uses them as a generic term for the little people:

> On Christmas-eve, in former days, the small people, or the spriggans, would meet at the bottom of the deepest mines, and have a midnight mass. Then those that were in the mine would hear voices, melodious beyond all earthly voices, singing 'Now well! now well!' (*The First Nowell*); and the strains of some deep-toned organ would shake the rocks. Of the grandeur of those meetings, old stories could not find words sufficiently sonorous to speak; it was therefore left to the imagination. But this was certain, the temple formed by the fairy bands in which to celebrate the eve of the birth of a Saviour, in whose mercy they all had hope, was of the most magnificent description.

From spriggans to humans, singing is natural to the Cornish. Hunt again, somewhat unkindly:

> Tradesmen have for the most part 'cacht their jobs', and the good house wife 'done her churs in season' on Christmas-eve. In many

families, a crock of 'fish and tatees' is discussed in West-Cornwall style before the 'singers' commence their time-honoured carol, 'While Shepherds', which is invariably sung to 'the same old tune', struck by some novice in *u* flat. There is usually a host of young men and maidens to accompany the 'singers'; these are composed of the choirs of two or three dissenting bodies, who chiefly select the members of their respective congregations for the honour of being disturbed from a sound nap on the eventful morning. The last two or three years the choirs have done their carolling amongst the most respectable of the inhabitants on the evening of Christmas-day, after divine service.

Margaret Courtney was more favourably disposed towards the old singers. She also remembered the little people:

The choir from the parish church and dissenting chapels go from house to house singing 'curls' (carols), for which they are given money or feasted; but the quaint old carols, 'The first good joy that Mary had', 'I saw three ships come sailing in', common forty years ago, are now never heard. The natives of Cornwall have been always famous for their carols; some of their tunes are very old. Even the Knockers, Sprig-gans, and all the underground spirits that may be always heard working where there is tin (and who are said to be the ghosts of the Jews who crucified Jesus), in olden times held mass and sang carols on Christmas-eve.

In the beginning of (thc ninctccnth) century at the ruined baptistry of St Levan.....all the carol-singers in that district, after visiting the neighbouring villages, met and sang together many carols. Mr Bottrell says, 'One was never forgotten, in which according to our West Country version, Holy Mary says to her dear Child:-

Go the wayst out, Child Jesus,
Go the wayst out to play;
Down by God's Holy Well
I see three pretty children
As ever tongue can tell.

This for its sweet simplicity is still a favourite in the west.
An old carol or ballad:

'Come and I will sing you,' etc.

known to many old people in all parts of the county, has been thought by some to be peculiar to Cornwall; but this is an error, as it has been heard elsewhere.

The first carol above is a version of *The Holy Well*, little known today, but collected by Cecil Sharp in Camborne in 1913. The second is presumably a fragment of *The Dilly Song*, better known as *Green Grow the Rushes-O*, still popular in junior schools: the late Peter Kennedy heard a good version in Launceston in 1950. It is ironic that the two carols forgotten in Courtney's time have now re-emerged, while the other two have virtually disappeared from public performance.

W.D. Watson, writing in *Old Cornwall* magazine for 1937, confirmed the deep significance of Christmas carols to the Cornish:

In conversing with an old inhabitant of Ludgvan parish at Christmas-time in 1935 on the subject of Cornish Christmas carols, he told me in connection with 'Hark What mean those Heavenly Voices?' a carol familiar to both of us, that when he was very young it was said that it was written 'in very ancient times, soon after

> the Christian religion was brought to Cornwall'. He had heard that on the night our Saviour was born, the Mousehole fishermen were coming home from sea, when early in the morning while they were still some miles from land a very brilliant light shone all around them and as far as their eyes could see. At the same time they heard most wonderful singing in the sky and they were all very astonished. When they came home they spread the news of these happenings, and years afterwards when the first Christian teachers came, telling the story of the Babe of Bethlehem, the fishermen were quite satisfied to accept the teaching, because they had seen and heard that some great thing had happened.

If the spirit of Christmas had begun to enter the lives of ordinary working people with this incident, it was an unstable benefit. Hunt quotes from the *St Ives Correspondent* for 1861, with an early knock at guising:

> We should not omit that one of the old customs still observed is the giving apprentices three clear holidays (not including Sunday) after Christmas-day, though we hear of attempts being made to lessen this treat to the youngsters. If we don't wish success to these efforts, we do desire those should succeed who will endeavour to impart to our rising population a thorough contempt for guise-dancing and all such unmeaning buffoonery.

This account by a North Hill resident, in the *Old Cornwall* magazine for 1938, splendidly evokes the dialect of east Bodmin Moor:

> FB told me that when a boy he lived on one of the moorland farms. Those were the days when Christmas was kept up in a good old style by moorland farmers, who visited each other in turn at their

> parties. 'I mm',' said he, 'ow us used to ev Chresmiss in they days. Us wud go wan plaice. One plaice was at Bastreet, ole M's varm. E'd maike 'aste and get 'is vrashin' done, and then 'e'd get 'is barn cleared out, all ready for the party, as the varm kitchen was tu smal'. They'd range the zacks round be the walls and they'd make purty zaits, tu zit on. There wud be dancin' and all zorts there gain on.' He also told how once a girl who was dancing had the misfortune to dance on a rotten part of the barn floor, and it gave away. One leg went through and she found herself standing on the back of a cow beneath!

Courtney, too, referred to parties, but for the New Year:

> Parties are general in Cornwall on New Year's-eve to watch in the New Year and wish friends health and happiness; but I know of no peculiar customs, except that before retiring to rest the old women opened their Bibles at hap-hazard to find out their luck for the coming year. The text on which the fore-finger of the right hand rested was supposed to foretell the future. And money, generally a piece of silver, was placed on the threshold, to be brought in the first thing on the following day, that there might be no lack of it for the year. Nothing was ever lent on New Year's-day, as little as possible taken out, but all that could be brought into the house.

She added Thomas Quiller Couch's comment that he had 'even known the dust of the floor swept inward', before continuing:

> Door-steps on New Year's-day were formerly sanded for good luck, because I suppose people coming into the house were sure to bring some of it in with them sticking to their feet.

Hunt expanded on this theme:

> In the rural districts of Cornwall, it is thought to be unlucky if a female is the first to enter the house on new-year's morning. To insure the contrary, it was customary to give boys some small reward for placing sand on the door-steps and in the passage.
>
> In many places, not many years since, droves of boys would march through the towns and villages, collecting their fees for 'sanding your steps for good luck'.

Courtney related another Cornish belief, harking back to a custom from at least the fifteenth century and which Thomas Hardy included in a poem about a Dorset Christmas:

> Many elderly people at the beginning of the (nineteenth) century still kept to the 'old style', and held their Christmas-day on Epiphany. On the eve of that day they said 'the cattle in the fields and stalls never lay down, but at midnight turned their faces to the east and fell on their knees'.

Hamilton Jenkin connected this belief with the burning of midwinter fires:

> In many cases the fires of Christmas were continued until Twelfth Night or 'Old Christmas Day'. It is recorded that about the year 1830 a number of Sennen farmers assembled on this occasion at a dinner of a 'four-and-twenty blackbird pie'. After the feast, some of the boldest of the young men went out at midnight in order to see the cattle kneel, facing the east. On their return they brought with them rushes which they threw on to the

> fire, and from the way in which these crackled or the particular form which they assumed in burning they told their fortunes for the ensuing year.
>
> It would certainly appear to be more than a coincidence that these ceremonial fires of midwinter should have so nearly corresponded with the season when the sun reaches its lowest elevation at noon, and, like the bonfires of midsummer, there is reason to suppose that they owed their origin to practices far older than the Christian festival with which they had become associated.

It is obvious that Twelfth Night was an important day in old Cornwall's folklore. Cattle again feature in a final recollection from the Liskeard area: on that day, cows should be fed a double ration of fodder or the farmer would suffer an avalanche of bad luck.

TWENTY YEARS AT ST HILARY

By Bernard Walke

Bernard Walke (1874-1941) was a high-Anglican and his early days as vicar of St Hilary, near Penzance, were fraught with difficulties and recalcitrant parishioners. He enjoyed the company of artists and writers and was particularly friendly with Compton Mackenzie, and it was, perhaps, his literary talent that finally won over his local critics. With his wife Annie, he wrote a Christmas play which became locally, then nationally, famous; the BBC broadcast it annually for many years. His fine autobiography *Twenty Years at St Hilary* was written in 1935. Like his eminent forebear Robert Stephen Hawker, he converted to Roman Catholicism just before his death.

The Christmas Play at St Hilary goes back so many years that I have almost forgotten its origin.

At the time I could find no play suitable to the place and the people who were to perform it. I wanted an act of worship rather than a performance, a return to the old miracle play which was performed either in the church or in some open space, such as the field known at St Hilary as the Plain-an-guarry, 'the field of the play'.

Even in the modern theatre where the stage is separated from the auditorium, the audience is so important a factor that I believe the most skilful producer cannot estimate the whole possibilities of a play before the first night, when the indefinable relationship between actors and spectators will often produce a new situation. It was this combined action of players and spectators that I was looking for. The old Cornish miracle plays appeared to me to be too archaic and lacking in dramatic form for my purpose; and finding nothing among the more modern plays that corresponded to my conception, I determined that if there was to be one at St Hilary it must be written by myself.

The plan with which I started was that there should be no stage and that the players should pass, as in a measured dance, from place to place round the church among the people. In addition I planned that the Christmas crib should take the place of a character impersonating Our Lady with the Holy Child, and that there should be a dance of children before the crib, as an expression of joy in the nativity.

I have often been weary of this play 'Bethlehem', which has been produced so many times and yet I never watch the grotesque figures of the shepherds with a fiddler at their head, followed by the children on their way to the dance before the crib, without experiencing a thrill of emotion. There is nothing in this crowd, in the music of the fiddler or the dances of the children, that is remotely related to the scene of the Nativity, and yet, as I watch them, I am more conscious of the joys of Christmas than I should be in witnessing the most realistic presentation.

I feel the same when the little girl arrives with the toy lamb in her arms. Children no longer care for woolly lambs as when I was a child. I searched the shops in Penzance to find one. 'We don't stock them,' was the answer I received. Teddy-bears were everywhere, but not a lamb to be found. At last I came upon a little toyshop kept by two old ladies in Market Jew Street. 'Yes,' said the elder of the two, who wore her hair in ringlets, 'I know what you want. Children used to be very fond of them when I was a girl, but we have not been asked for such a thing in years. Fancy now! children like one of these things,' she went on, pointing to a yellow Teddy-bear with a pink ribbon round its neck, 'rather than a little white lamb.' 'I do believe,' said the younger woman, 'we still have one put away somewhere. If the gentleman doesn't mind waiting we might find it. Or perhaps you will call again?' she said. I determined to wait while the old ladies busied themselves in turning out cupboards and peeping into boxes. At last, when all the cupboards had been emptied out, a lamb was found in a box on the top shelf, a woolly lamb with crooked legs and a bell round its neck. I have never looked on greater innocency. 'We won't charge you the full price,' they said, 'for no one wants them to-day.' I am glad that others loved the lamb as I did. Gert Harvey, a painter in Newlyn, came to me after the play. 'O Ber,' she said, where did you get that lamb? His crooked legs made me cry.'

It must be fifteen years ago since I first produced the play 'Bethlehem'. In fifteen years there is much change in the life of a village. Many have died and not a few have been born. Of the players themselves, those who were children and danced in the play have grown to men and women, some with children of their own, but the play continues unchanged and has become part of the tradition of St Hilary.

CAROL FOR TWELFTH DAY

This fine, if little known, secular carol was collected early in the nineteenth century by the antiquary Davies Gilbert, originally Giddy, who was born at St Erth in 1767. Known as 'The Cornish Philosopher', Gilbert was a diligent collector, generous with his knowledge, who sponsored great men of his day, including Sir Humphry Davy. He published *The Parochial History of Cornwall* in 1838 and died a year later.

Sweet master of this habitation with my mistress be so kind
As to grant an invitation if we may this favour find
To be invited in then with mirth we will begin
Happy, sweet and pleasant songs which unto this time belongs.
Let every loyal, honest soul contribute to the wassail bowl!

So may you still enjoy the blessing of a loving, virtuous wife;
Riches, honour, still possessing with a long and happy life:
Living in prosperity then let generosity
Always be maintained, I pray, don't forget the good old way.
Let every loyal, honest soul contribute to the wassail bowl!

Before the season is departed in your presence we appear:
Therefore soon be noble-hearted to afford some dainty cheer.
Freely let us have it now since the season does allow;
What thc house does now afford should be placed upon the board,
Whether it be roast beef or fowl and liquor well the wassail bowl!

For now it is a time of leisure, then to those that kindness show:
May they have wealth, peace and pleasure and the spring of
bounty flow,
To enrich them while they live that they may afford to give
To maintain the good old way many a long and happy day.
Let every loyal, honest soul contribute to the wassail bowl!

You worthy are to be commended if in this you will not fail;
Now our song is almost ended fill our bowl with nappy ale:
Then we'll drink a full carouse to the master of this house,
Aye and to our mistress dear, wishing both a happy year,
In peace and love without control who brought joy to our wassail bowl!

'Nappy' ale, incidentally, was a strong, frothy beer.

WASSAIL!

Wassail, from the Anglo-Saxon *waes hael*, 'be of good health', has come to mean a general merrymaking. It originated, though, in the old Christmas or New Year custom where groups of revellers paraded through towns and villages carrying bowls from which they distributed hot alcoholic drink, perhaps lamb's wool, a form of punch made with hot ale, spices, sugar, roasted apples, eggs and cream. As Christina Hole has noted, their actions 'were not entirely altruistic', as the songs which accompanied these libations always included a direct request for food, drink or money. Fruit orchards were wassailed, too, invoking the gods to produce a successful harvest.

In her *Folklore and Customs of Rural England* (1974), Margaret Baker wrote:

> Wassailing is in village pasts, but one group led by Harold Tozer, who has wassailed for over sixty years, carries the traditional bowl, decorated with mistletoe and ribbons, to inns and farms round Truro ... just as the exiled Cornish miners did in nineteenth-century Butte, Montana.

Sadly, the custom in Truro has now died out, as it has in many other Cornish towns and villages. A.K. Hamilton Jenkin, writing in 1934, describes wassailing, including a song from Stithians, which is almost identical to that sung in the 1950s by the late Charlie Bate and residents of St Merryn, near Padstow. Similar versions were collected in Fowey, Jacobstow, Grampound, Tregony and elsewhere.

> In Cornwall the bowl, generally made of wood, was decorated and looped around with furze blossom, flowers, ivy, and ribbons. Armed with this magnificent trophy, the wassailers visited the neighbouring farms and houses of the gentry, before whose doors they struck up the following song:
>
> The mistress and master our warzail begin,
> Pray open your door and let us come in,
> With our warzail, warzail, warzail, warzail,
> And joy come to our jolly warzail.
>
> The mistress and master sitting down by the fire
> While we poor warzailers are travelling the mire,
> With our warzail, etc.
>
> The mistress and master sitting down at their ease,
> Put their hands in their pockets and give what they please,
> For our warzail, etc.
> I hope that your apple trees will prosper and bear
> That we may have cider when we come next year,
> With our warzail, etc.
>
> And where you've one hogshead, I hope you'll have ten,
> That we may have cider when we come again,
> With our warzail, etc.

I hope that your barley will prosper and grow,
That you may have some and enough to bestow
On our warzail, etc.

Now we poor warzail boys growing weary and old,
Drop a small bit of silver into our bowl,
For our warzail, etc.

I wish you a blessing and a long time to live,
Since you've been so free and so willing to give
To our warzail, etc.

At the conclusion of the ceremony, as the song suggests, the wassailers were assured of a warm welcome, which generally took the form of a glass of 'shenagrum' and a slice of the Christmas cake.

The latter is still a regular feature of the Christmastide in Cornwall, and there will hardly be found a cottage, however poor, which does not attempt to provide something of the sort at this season for the entertainment of chance visitors.

Shenagrum was usually prepared by bringing half a pint of home-brewed beer to the boil, then adding to it a half noggin of pure Jamaica rum, a slice of lemon, with soft brown sugar and grated nutmeg to taste. Served either hot or cold, the drink was known variously as 'schnagrum', 'schnack' or 'shenackerum', explained by Robert Morton Nance as a distortion of the once-familiar dog-Latin expression 'super naculum': 'on the nail'.

Over forty years before Hamilton Jenkin was writing, Margaret Courtney included the following notes on wassailing from an anonymous farmer from mid-Cornwall who had spoken with Thomas Quiller Couch in 1883:

> In some places the parishioners walk in procession, visiting the principal orchards in the parish. In each orchard one tree is selected, as the representative of the rest; this is saluted with a certain form of words, which have in them the form of an incantation. They then sprinkle the tree with cider, or dash a bowl of cider against it, to ensure its bearing plentifully the ensuing year. In other places the farmers and their servants only assemble on the occasion, and after immersing apples in cider hang them on the apple-trees. They then sprinkle the trees with cider; and after uttering a formal incantation, they dance round it (or rather round them), and return to the farmhouse to conclude these solemn rites with copious draughts of cider.
>
> In Warleggan, on Christmas-eve, it was customary for some of the household to put in the fire (bank it up), and the rest to take a jar of cider, a bottle, and a gun to the orchard, and put a small bough into the bottle. Then they said:-

Here's to thee, old apple-tree!
Hats full, packs full, great bushel-bags full!
Hurrah! and fire off the gun.

A similar incantation is still used today at the wassail ceremony in Carhampton, Somerset. Courtney continues:

> The words chanted in East Cornwall were:-
>
> Health to thee, good apple-tree,
> Pocket-fulls, hat-fulls, peck-fulls, bushel-bag-fulls.

Word construction obviously degenerated towards the Tamar. Courtney also noted wassail bowl ceremonies in east Cornwall:

> On New Year's-eve ... soon after dusk, parties of men, from four to six in a party, carrying a small bowl in their hands, went from house to house begging money to make a feast. They opened the doors without knocking, called out Warsail, and sang ...
>
> These poor jolly Warsail boys
> Come travelling through the mire.
>
> This custom was common fifty years since, and may still be observed in remote rural districts.

In Bodmin today the custom lives on. The Bodmin Wassailers, clad in gentlemen's 'hand-me-downs', with top hats and flowery waistcoats, carry their bowl and collecting-box through the town every Twelfth Night; they walk from door to door, singing:

Our Wassail Bowl is full with apples and good spice,
Grant to taste it once or twice,
And joy come to our jolly wassail.

These days, they collect for charity rather than the alehouse.

ON THE THIRTEENTH DAY OF CHRISTMAS

By Charles Causley

Charles Causley, the finest British ballad poet of his generation was born in 1917 in Launceston, where he lived for most of his life. Before the Second World War, he worked as a builder's clerk, then enlisted in the Royal Navy, which inspired many of his poems and short stories. After the war, he became a primary-school teacher, a career he embraced until retirement. He immersed himself in Cornish culture, never lost his native accent and played piano in a country dance band during the 1950s. A committed Christian, he died in 2003, probably one of Britain's best-loved poets. Perhaps, he, too, should have become Poet Laureate, but what would that have done to his talent?

On the thirteenth day of Christmas
I saw King Jesus go
About the plain beyond the pane
Wearing his cap of snow.

Sad was his brow as the snow-sky
While all the world made merry,
In the black air the wounds burned bare
As the fire in the holly berry.

At all the weeping windows
The greedy children gather
And laugh at the clown in his white nightgown
In the wicked winter weather.

I dragged the desperate city,
I swagged the combing light,
I stood alone at the empty throne
At the ninth hour of night.

On the thirteenth day of Christmas
When the greasy guns bellow
His eye is dry as the splitting sky
And his face is yellow.

BIBLIOGRAPHY

Acton, Viv and Bob: *A History of Truro*, Volume 2, 2002
Baker, Margaret: *Folklore and Customs of Rural England*, 1974
Baring-Gould, Sabine: *The Vicar of Morwenstow*, 1876
Bonham, Mrs John: *Christmas in Cornwall 60 Years Ago*, 1898
Bottrell, William: *Traditions and Hearthside Stories of West Cornwall*, 1880
Brice, Douglas: *The Folk Carol of England*, 1967
Brittain, F.: *Q Anthology*, 1948
Burton, Anthony: *Richard Trevithick: Giant of Steam*, 2002
Causley, Charles: *Collected Poems*, 1992
Clemo, Jack: *The Clay Verge*, 1951
Couch, Jonathan: *The History of Polperro*, 1871
Courtney, M.A.: *Cornish Feasts and Folklore*, 1890
Deane, Tony and Shaw, Tony: *Folklore of Cornwall*, 2003
Dearmer, Percy and others: *The Oxford Book of Carols*, 1928 & *revised edition*, 1987
Douch, H.L.: *Old Cornish Inns*, 1966
Du Maurier, Daphne: *Vanishing Cornwall*, 1966
Dunstan, Ralph: *The Cornish Song Book*, 1929
Dunstan, Ralph: *Cornish Dialect and Folk Songs*, 1932
Edwards, Thornton B: *Cornish!*, 2005
Forrest, John: *The History of Morris Dancing* 1458-1750, 1999
Gundry, Inglis: *Canow Kernow*, 1966
Hamilton Jenkin, A K: *Cornish Homes and Customs*, 1934
Hocking, Salome: *Some Old Cornish Folk*, 1903

Hole, Christina: *A Dictionary of British Folk Customs*, 1976
Hunt, Robert: *Popular Romances of the West of England*, 1881
Hutton, Patrick: *I Would Not Be Forgotten*, 2004
Kennedy, Peter & others: *Folksongs of Britain and Ireland*, 1975
Kent, Alan M.: *The Literature of Cornwall*, 2000
Lakeman, Mary: *Early Tide: A Mevagissey Childhood*, 1978
Marsden, Philip: *The Main Cages*, 2002
Paynter, S. Winifred: *Old St Ives: The Reminiscences of William Paynter*, 1927
Phillipps, K.C.: *The Cornish Journal of Charles Lee*, 1995
Pryor, Oswald: *Australia's Little Cornwall*, 1962
Rees, Edgar A.: *Old Penzance*, 1956
Routley, Erik: *The English Carol*, 1958
Rowse, A.L.: *A Cornish Childhood*, 1942
Rowse, A.L.: *A Life: Collected Poems*, 1981
Rowse, A.L.: *Quiller Couch: A Portrait of Q*, 1988
Smelt, Maurice: 101 *Cornish Lives*, 2006
Smith, Chris: *A West Country Christmas*, 1989
Tregarthen, J.C.: *John Penrose*, 1923
Treneer, Anne: *Schoolhouse in the Wind*, 1944
Vyvyan, C.C.: *Our Cornwall*, 1948
Vyvyan, C.C.: *A Cornish Year*, 1958
Walke, Bernard: *Twenty Years at St Hilary*, 1935
Whetter, James: *Essays Ancient and Modern*, 2005
Worden, John: *Strike Sound: Padstow Carols*, 1971

Newspapers

The Guardian, *The Times*, *The West Briton*

Periodicals

An Baner Kernewek (The Cornish Banner), *The Cornish Magazine* (Nineteenth century series), *Old Cornwall*

INDEX OF EXTRACTS